Finding the One

A 1960s Love Story

Lisa Boatman

Copyright © 2025 by Lisa Boatman

All rights reserved.
No part of this book may be reproduced, stored in a retrieval system, or transmitted in any form or by any means - electronic, mechanical, photocopying, recording, or otherwise - without prior written permission from the publisher, except by a reviewer who may quote brief passages in a review.

First Edition
Printed in the United States of America

ISBN: 979-8-218-75192-0 (paperback)
(Also available in eBook at Amazon Kindle)

Cover design by Lisa Boatman
All illustrations by Lisa Boatman (courtesy of Canva)
Editor and layout by Ingrid Delle Jacobson

Dedication

To my parents, Karen and Howard Boatman, who celebrated 60 years of marriage on August 21, 2025.

Table of Contents

Dedication iii
Prologue vii
Chapter 1 1
Chapter 2 45
Chapter 3 67
Chapter 4 93
Chapter 5 127
Chapter 6 191
Chapter 7 211
Chapter 8 245
Chapter 9 259
Chapter 10 275
Chapter 11 293
Epilogue 314
About the Author 316

Prologue

In the digital era, the search for love often resembles online car shopping. People scour their phones, seeking the perfect "model" based on curated appearances and profiles, and initially experience intense infatuation. However, this superficial approach can lead to a cycle of failed relationships, revealing a critical loss of genuine connection that struggles to thrive in our technologically saturated society.

"There is hardly any activity that started with such tremendous hopes and expectations and yet fails so regularly as love" – Erich Fromm.

In the 1960s, most people didn't have this perspective. True romantic success, as our elders understood, doesn't stem from chasing superficial ideals of appearance or personality profiles. Instead, it blossoms from within. Building meaningful relationships necessitates a strong foundation of self-qualities: a profound understanding of oneself, a caring nature, a deep respect for others, a sense of responsibility, an unwavering commitment, boundless patience, and the willingness and ability to compromise. Love is a leap of faith, built on trust that your partner will be there for you when you need them most.

If you can't embody these principles within yourself, how can you expect someone to love you?

Chapter 1

As the summer sun cast long, hazy shadows on their street, a black sedan with an Illinois state seal emblazoned on the side eased into their driveway.

"They're here, Porter," Olga cried out from the bay window as she watched the driver park and walk around to the back of the sedan. Porter strode into the living room, wrapping his arms around her. They watched as their social worker carried a baby toward the front door.

Porter greeted them at the door with a warm smile. The humid Illinois summer surged into the house with the social worker and driver, and Porter quickly shut the door to keep it cool.

The Smiths had endured a relentless gauntlet of challenges: countless medical appointments and months grappling with infertility. Then came the bureaucratic labyrinth of adoption paperwork and evaluations, each step pushing them toward an uncertain future. Yet, after ten long years, they had persevered, arriving at this pivotal moment in their lives.

Olga froze as Porter gazed at the baby in the social worker's arms.

"She's beautiful, Olga. Come here and see," he said, smiling at Olga.

Olga remained stiff, her eyes fixed on the baby but not truly seeing her. The social worker, noticing Olga's subtle withdrawal, decided to approach her. Olga's face lit up with a mother's smile as her eyes admired the baby's tiny, rounded cheeks, full lips, and downy brown hair. "Meet your daughter, Karen."

A single tear rolled down Olga's face as she looked back at her husband.

"Can I hold her?" Olga asked as the social worker handed her baby over. Karen was momentarily disturbed from her deep sleep but quickly returned to a peaceful slumber. Olga cradled her in her arms, mesmerized by the peacefulness of her sleep. She gently touched her soft face, feeling an overwhelming sense of contentment.

"She has a lot of hair for six months, don't you think, Olga?" the social worker asked.

"Yeah," she whispered, brushing her fingers across the silky baby hair on the top of her head.

"Where are the grandparents?" the social worker asked, looking at Porter.

Chapter 1

"Walter Nycell died today, so Olga's dad couldn't get away. Olga's mother is on her way over now," Porter said.

"Yes, I heard he passed this afternoon. Did he go to your father's church?" she asked Olga.

"He served as an usher for 25 years. He used to give me candy when I was little. He was a very nice man."

"Oh, really? My dad was an usher, too, before he joined the Navy."

"Where is he now?" Porter asked.

"He is stationed under MacArthur in the Pacific aboard the USS South Dakota."

After a few minutes of polite goodbyes and well wishes, the social worker and driver stepped out into the August heat. Olga and Porter's gazes were fixed on the black sedan as it smoothly backed down the driveway, leaving them alone with the incredible, quiet weight of Olga's arms.

"What do we do now?" Porter asked as they looked at each other.

"The best we can, I guess."

"Blow out the candles, Karen!" one of her friends yelled. With a big smile, Karen leaned forward and blew out the seven flickering candles on the rich, double-layer chocolate cake, prompting cheerful applause from her friends. Dressed in a sparkling Cinderella costume, complete with a shimmering tiara and wand, she was the undeniable belle of the ball.

After the birthday cake, Olga and Porter directed the girls to open presents. Karen and her friends always played Ginnies, so most gifts were outfits and accessories.

After she finished opening all her gifts, Porter came out with one last present.

"What is it, Dad?" she asked.

"Open it and find out!" he replied with a wink.

She ripped off the wrapping paper from the gift as the girls gasped in unison. In her hands was the must-have dress of the season—the beautiful Afternoon Tea Party Ginny dress. She lifted it out of the box, careful not to rip the dress. The soft fabric draped gracefully like a gentle breeze as she showcased it to everyone, her eyes shining with joy.

As the other girls surrounded Karen to look at the dress, she handed it off and ran to Porter and Olga, giving him a big hug.

"*Thank* you!"

Chapter 1

After opening the presents, the girls played hide-and-seek in the basement while Olga and Porter cleaned up the mess. After a fun afternoon, one by one, the girls left for supper.

"Karen, it's time for your piano lesson!" Olga announced after they finished dessert. Each night after supper, they practiced together. They started with scales to warm up, then Karen played pieces from her Intermediate Piano book while her mother watched. She maintained good timing and made rapid progress in her music reading skills.

"Mom, do you think I can play for the church one day?" she asked.

"Well, you will have to talk to your grandfather about that," Olga said. "But if you keep practicing your skills, I think he might find a place for you in the service someday."

One cold, February morning, Karen and her friends were walking to school together.

"Karen, can we play Ginnies at your house after school?" Georgene said.

"Yeah, I want to come over, too!" Pam chimed in.

"Great idea!"

After school, the three friends transformed the basement into an imaginary world. They created a volleyball net from wooden Tinker Toys. Berry-Blue Kool-Aid granules formed a shimmering 'ocean,' while short rulers served as surfboards. Mid-game, Georgene, laughing, slipped on a patch of Kool-Aid, tumbling headfirst onto the makeshift beach. A sickening *rip* echoed through the room as Karen's Ginny doll, dressed in her brand-new dress, lay mangled. Georgene's laughter instantly dissolved into a wail, and Karen and Pam scrambled to her side.

Seconds later, Olga rushed downstairs. A large, angry lump bloomed on Georgene's forehead, but there was thankfully no blood. Olga called Georgene's mom, who arrived within minutes to collect her.

"I'm so sorry I ripped her dress," Georgene said through her sobs.

"That's okay. Maybe my mom can fix it," Karen replied.

Georgene protested, "But it's your favorite, Karen?"

Karen grabbed her hand and said, "I'm more worried about you."

Chapter 1

Three years later, Karen's grandfather asked her a question during Sunday dinner. "Karen, do you remember Mrs. Kimball from church?"

"Yes, she was my preschool teacher. She taught us Bible stories."

"Well, Mrs. Kimball is retiring next month from the church staff, so there's an opening for her preschool class. Would you like to teach the preschoolers during the service?"

Karen stared at her grandfather with wide eyes. "Yes, I would!"

"It's a lot of work and a big responsibility for a 10-year-old. You need to prepare a weekly lesson plan that includes storytelling for children aged three, four, and five years old."

"I can do it!" Karen said.

"You will need some assistance at first. I'll discuss this with Mrs. Kimball. Both of you can develop a lesson plan during this transition."

"Yes, and I'll help, too," Olga replied. "I'll take you to the church for the meetings with Mrs. Kimball, and I'll help you prepare for your class."

"Can I play the piano during class, Grandpa? I have some ideas for adding music to the lesson plan with the preschoolers."

The pastor thought for a second. "If the piano does not compete with my sermon, then yes, of course."

A few weeks later, during her final preschool class, Mrs. Kimball talked with Olga after the service.

"Honestly, Olga, I was skeptical when Pastor Swanson suggested his ten-year-old granddaughter take over my preschool class. But Karen is such a responsible and ambitious young lady! The students have really taken a liking to her. She relates to them, something I struggle with in my 70s. I feel very confident in her ability to lead this class."

"Thank you, Mrs. Kimball," Olga replied. "We appreciate the confidence you have shown in her, too. Over the last month, she has proven to Pastor Swanson and me that she takes this role seriously. Did she tell you she uses Ginnies for students when preparing her lesson? It's adorable! Anyway, I will observe her during class for the first few weeks in case she has problems."

"Good idea, Olga. And thank you for your support, too."

"Vasco de Gama was a Portuguese explorer who was the first European to discover the sea route to India from Europe in 1499," Karen said.

"How can I remember that date?" Pam asked.

"Well, it was seven years after Columbus discovered the New World, so how about a rhyme, like…" Karen thought for a moment. "Seven years after Christopher Columbus, Vasco de Gama found India with a compass."

"Hey, that's pretty good! And easy to remember, too," Pam said, smiling at her. "Thanks for taking the time to help me today. I'm having so much trouble remembering these dates for history class."

"Of course, Pam! That's what friends do."

"But Karen, you not only help me—you help everyone in the 7th grade. Why do you do it?"

"God says, 'Do unto others as you would have them do unto you,'" she replied. "Someday, I might need some help with my homework, too. Like learning all those acids and bases in chemistry class!"

"Oh, I don't like that class, either. You should make up a rhyme to remember that stuff!"

After finishing her piano practice with Olga one evening, Karen went to her bedroom and began

Chapter 1

working on her Sunday school lesson about David and Goliath. A few minutes later, her parents came into the room and sat on the bed.

"We want to tell you how special you are, Karen," Olga began. "You are 13 years old now, and it's time you knew the truth."

Karen closed her picture book and looked at Olga. "The truth about what, Mom?"

"You see, Karen, sometimes moms and dads can't have children. They go to a special place to find a child if they want a family."

"Where is that?"

"It's called an adoption center."

Karen thought for a moment. "Yeah, I've heard of that. One of my classmates is adopted. He once stood up in class and said he had two parents: biological and adoptive."

Olga and Porter exchanged looks. Olga placed her hands over Karen's and said, "Karen, you have two sets of parents too."

Karen's stare drilled into Olga, trying to decipher the meaning behind her words. A slow, bewildered blink punctuated the silence.

"Wait," she asked, her voice hushed, "does that mean I also came from the adoption center?"

"Yes, dear," Porter's voice was gentle and understanding. Olga nodded her head, too.

Karen looked down at her lap, with Olga's hand over hers, feeling the weight of the moment. Her heart thumped in her chest as she asked, "So, you're not my real parents?"

"No, we are your parents—your adoptive parents," Porter confirmed.

"Okay, can I meet my birth parents?"

Olga hesitated. "No, you can't."

"Why not?"

"Honey, we don't know who they are," Olga said.

"Why not?"

Olga looked at Porter and said, "Because they don't want you in their lives."

Karen yanked her hands from Olga's grasp, her eyes blazing red as they pierced hers. "Why *not*?" she hissed, the question laced with venom.

Porter tried to explain, "Your biological parents had a very good reason for giving you up for adoption."

"What's the reason? What did they tell you?"

"There's nothing more we can tell you, dear," Olga said, her voice soft but firm. "You need to accept that."

"But I want to meet my mom and dad!"

Olga touched her arm. "Honey, *we* are your mom and dad."

Chapter 1

"No, you're not. You're my adoptive parents. I want to meet my birth parents."

"Karen, do you remember how we taught you to bake cookies, gave you ideas for Bible stories to teach to your class, and bought you everything you wanted on your birthday and at Christmas?" Olga said. "Why don't you see us as your parents?"

Karen hesitated, then said, "You're not my mother. You didn't give birth to me."

Olga buried her face in her hands and fled, shaking as she stumbled out of her room.

"Well, you didn't," she yelled after Olga in the hallway.

"Karen, go apologize to your mother right now," Porter said.

"No, if anyone should apologize, it's her. How could she not know who my birth parents are? That's so unfair. She knows who *her* parents are!"

That night, Karen tossed and turned in her sleep. *How could Mom be so irresponsible as not to know my birth parents?* she thought. This felt very unfair. They could have at least asked them their names. Maybe she could find out who they are? Perfect! She could go to the adoption center and ask!

Karen didn't wait for her alarm. She sprang from bed, dressing with practiced speed. No usual morning rituals, no mumbled farewells; she bolted out the door, her mind consumed by one pressing question. If she hurried, she might uncover her birth parents' names before the 8:30 a.m. school bell.

"May I help you, young lady?" asked the social worker as Karen arrived promptly at 8 a.m.

"Yes, my name is Karen Smith. I want to know who my birth parents are."

"Yes, I remember you—you're Paster Swenson's granddaughter. I delivered you to your parents."

"Olga and Porter are not my parents," Karen insisted.

The social worker looked at Karen for a moment. "I see. Well, let me check your file and see what we can find about your biological parents." She left and returned with a file, glancing at it briefly. Karen watched her with wide eyes. "Hmm, it says here you have a closed adoption."

"What does that mean?" Karen asked.

"It means your biological parents do not want to identify themselves."

"Can I open a closed adoption?"

The social worker smiled as she closed the folder. "No, dear. No one can do that now."

Chapter 1

"But I want to meet them. How do I do that?"

"Well," she frowned at Karen, "you can't, dear."

"Okay, well, I want to contact them. What are their names? I'll find them in the phone book." Karen reached for her pen and paper from her backpack.

"Karen, I'm sorry, but I cannot tell you that."

"You can't even tell me their names? They are my parents, and everyone has the right to know who their parents are."

"Karen, I'm sorry."

"This isn't fair," Karen pouted. "I'm their daughter! You have to tell me!"

The social worker met Karen's defiant gaze, her lips pressed into a thin, unyielding line. The information Karen so desperately craved remained hidden, ensnared in a web of confidentiality clauses and legal precedents that bound the social worker's tongue. Karen let out a harsh, disbelieving snort. With a frustrated growl, she spun and stormed out.

After she left, the social worker picked up the phone.

As the girls left school, one of them asked, "Why are we going to your grandparents' house today, Karen?"

"Well… last night, Olga and Porter told me I was adopted. I don't want to see them."

"You're adopted? Really?" Pam asked with a funny look.

"Yeah, I am," Karen replied, looking dejected as they made their way to her grandparents' house.

Georgene touched her arm. "Are you okay?"

"No, not really," Karen replied. "I went to the adoption center this morning before school. She wouldn't tell me who my birth parents are or even give me their names."

"That's terrible!" said Georgene. "Why not?"

"I don't know, but I think it's related to Olga and Porter. They don't want me to find out."

They arrived at Karen's grandparents' house a few minutes later.

"Have you heard about this new singer, Elvis?" one girl asked.

Everyone got excited, including Karen. She had just heard *Heartbreak Hotel* on the radio the other day. "I've heard he is captivating to watch," Karen said, a mischievous grin spreading on her face.

Chapter 1

Her grandparents' house welcomed them with open arms. Kicks sent the can rattling down the pavement, followed by a chorus of shouts and giggles. Then, the rhythmic slap of jump ropes against concrete filled the air. As their initial burst of energy waned, the games shifted to hushed counts behind bushes for hide-and-seek, broken later by sharp commands of "Red light!" and breathless sprints. A faint aroma of supper cooking drifted from open kitchen windows, and soon, one by one, her friends drifted away.

Karen went inside and asked her grandmother, "Can I stay for supper tonight?"

"Of course, dear."

During supper, her grandfather asked Karen, "Your mother tells me you argued yesterday. Can you tell me what happened?"

"Grandpa, they told me I am adopted, and they don't know who my parents are."

"Well, your parents are your mom and dad."

"No, Grandpa. They are my adoptive parents. Olga didn't give birth to me."

Her grandfather's face grew stern. "Karen, calling your mother by her first name is disrespectful."

"But other kids do it. There's a boy in my class who was adopted, and he calls his adopted parents by their first names."

"You will stop calling your mother by her first name."

"Yes, sir," Karen replied. "But Grandpa, the Bible teaches us not to lie. I feel like she lied to me about who I am. How can I trust her anymore?"

"Your mother loves you very much; she always has. You need to trust both her and your father because they know what is best for you," he said, looking at her intently. "What is the Fifth Commandment, Karen?"

"Love your father and mother, sir."

"That doesn't mean sometimes; it means all the time."

"Yes, sir," Karen replied, looking disappointed.

"After we eat, we'll drive you home and talk to your mother together. You need to apologize for what you said. She is heartbroken."

"Yes, sir."

The next night, Olga and Karen did the dishes after supper.

"Karen, I went to the music store today and bought some new Bible songs for your class on Sunday. Shall we try them after we finish the dishes? I think you will like them!"

Chapter 1

"No, thank you," Karen said sullenly.

"Well, we will just go over your lessons, then."

"I don't feel like it tonight."

"But... we practice every night after supper."

"Sorry, but I have homework to do. I also need to prepare for my lesson on Sunday. I'm not that interested in playing piano anymore."

"Okay..." Olga said, her voice trailing off as Karen ran to her bedroom.

Months later, the melody of Georgene's new violin continued to stir a deep longing within Karen. *Someday, maybe,* she wished, clinging to the fragile hope that Porter and Olga might approve a violin for her, too.

One night, during the murmurs of conversation at supper, her courage began to solidify. Finally, the burden too heavy to bear, the question burst from her lips. "Um, can I have a violin?"

Olga asked, "What about piano?"

"I don't want to play piano anymore."

Olga sighed. "But violins are expensive."

Georgene had shown her how to beg because it worked for her. "Pleeeease!" she said, stretching out the word and looking at her dad. "Georgene has one."

Olga and Porter exchanged glances. Finally, Porter said, "Okay, we will go down to Guzzardo's and see what they have in stock after supper."

"Oh, thank you!" Karen cried.

Guzzardo's Music Store was the go-to place for everything related to music. They had records, sheet music, pianos, and musical instruments. When they arrived, Karen rushed to the string instrument section and began examining their selection.

"May I help you, young lady?" inquired Mr. Guzzardo.

"Yes, sir. I'd like to look at your violins, please," Karen replied.

"Well, these are the violas. The violin selection is there," he said as he pointed to the violins. He smiled at Olga and Porter as they looked on.

"Excuse me, what's the difference? Violins look exactly like violas?" she asked.

"You're right. They do look similar, don't they?" He pulled down one of the violins and handed it to her, then grabbed a viola and bow. "Violas have a slightly larger body, which gives them a richer and deeper

Chapter 1

sound than a violin." Mr. Guzzardo then held up a viola next to the violin. "Do you see the size difference?"

"Yes, I see it now," she replied.

Mr. Guzzardo nestled the instrument beneath his chin and drew a bow across the viola. He played the opening of William Walton's Viola Concerto. Karen's fifteen-year-old gaze clung to him as if each note physically pulled her deeper into the music.

"Wow! You are terrific!" Karen said after he stopped playing. Olga and Porter clapped, and Mr. Guzzardo bowed slightly.

"Thank you, young lady," he replied. "You see, the difference is in the thickness of the strings. Hold up your violin again," he asked, placing the viola beside it. "See how the viola's strings are thicker?"

"Yes, I see it," Karen replied.

"Because it produces lower notes, the viola is played in alto clef, not treble clef," Mr. Guzzardo said.

"Excuse me, Mr. Guzzardo, but don't you mean bass clef?"

"No, I mean alto clef. Let me guess, you play piano, right?"

Karen smiled, "Yes, how did you know?"

"Alto clef is used with only a few instruments, including the viola. The violin you are holding uses treble clef."

"Can I try to play your viola, Mr. Guzzardo?" Karen asked, holding out her violin. They exchanged instruments, and Mr. Guzzardo showed her how to hold it up to her neck and held out the bow.

"Now, when you hold the bow, bend your thumb and place it between the bow and the frog, then put your first three fingers on the base of the bow, like this."

A few minutes later, Karen was playing scales on her viola under Mr. Guzzardo's watchful eye. He stood beside Olga and Porter as she performed.

"And she's never played viola before?" Mr. Guzzardo asked.

"Not that I'm aware of," Olga said as Karen continued.

"Most beginners struggle with scales, but she's mastered them without any practice."

"She played piano for years," Olga beamed.

"What is your name, young lady?" Mr. Guzzardo asked.

"Karen Smith."

Mr. Guzzardo crouched down and looked her in the eye. "Karen, I teach viola to students here in the store. You have impressed me with your musical skills on the viola. I have openings on Tuesdays and Fridays at 4 p.m. Would you like me to teach you to play the viola?"

Chapter 1

"Well, let me ask my dad," she urged, her eyes wide as she stared at Porter with a silent, desperate hope.

"Of course, Mr. Guzzardo," Porter replied.

Although she didn't get a violin like Georgene did, they both enjoyed playing music together. Karen provided the lower counterpoint to Georgene's higher-pitched violin. For years, they enjoyed practicing together in their parents' basements.

The Fall Recital was only two days away. Today, the orchestra and choir convened for the final rehearsal. Karen, a junior now in her third year with the orchestra, occupied the first viola chair. Her best friend, Georgene, played in the violin section. The recital program featured a duet spotlighting Karen and the choir's first alto.

After the choir and orchestra finished their run-through, the soloists were asked to stay behind so they could practice their duets with their partners. Karen waved goodbye to Georgene as she left.

A handsome young man walked over with the choir teacher. "John, you will be singing your part with Karen. Karen is first viola for the orchestra."

"Nice to meet you, Karen," John said, extending his sweaty hand.

Karen was captivated by his good looks. She had seen him around school a few times. She was glad she'd worn her favorite plaid skirt that day. She took his hand. He had soft hands for a boy. "Nice to meet you, too," she said, smiling at him. Karen crossed her legs as John sat down next to her.

"Umm… how are you?" John fumbled a little with his words.

"Okay, I guess," Karen said.

John looked up and said, "I've seen you before around school. You hang out with Georgene, right?"

"Yes, she's my best friend. We have known each other since we were little."

"Yeah, she's nice," he stammered, the simple phrase hanging in the air as he grasped for a follow-up.

"How long have you played viola?"

"About three years. Mr. Guzzardo at the music store is my teacher."

"Hey, that's my dad!" he said.

"Your dad is Mr. Guzzardo? He never told me about you. He's very good at the viola."

Chapter 1

"Yes, he played for years with the Illinois Chamber Orchestra when he met my mom. After they got married, we moved to Rockford, and he opened the store."

"Yeah, he told me he played in an orchestra…" she said, her voice trailing off as they both looked down at their shoes.

"Maybe we should practice now?" Karen looked up and smiled.

Within minutes, Karen recognized his tells: the tapping foot, the rapid blinking, and the tightening jaw when he missed his note. *Just like Mr. Guzzardo*, her mind whispered. A quiet amusement curved her lips as she met his eye.

They practiced for another hour. Neither of them wanted to stop.

"Karen, we make beautiful music together," John said as his face flushed red.

Karen smiled at him. "Yes, we do! You have a wonderful singing voice. I sing a little, too. I was a Sunday school teacher for six years at my grandfather's church in Durand."

"Really?" John replied. "Let's hear you sing!"

"No, I can't," Karen smiled, looking away and blushing.

Chapter 1

"Please? For me?" John begged.

Karen shrugged, "Alright, I'll sing you one of the songs I used to sing to my preschool students at my grandpa's church."

Karen serenaded John with *Jesus Loves Me*. His eyes never left her as a smile spread across his face.

When her voice faded, he murmured, "A beautiful song from a beautiful girl." Karen's head bowed, a rosy flush creeping up her neck.

"Would you like to go to The Last Straw after practice for a malt?" John asked.

Karen's face lit up. "I would love to!"

She gazed at John as he disappeared down the sidewalk, leaving Karen beaming on her doorstep after their first kiss. She floated inside, a vast grin stretching across her face, her chest still pulsing with the evening's magic.

"It's 8 p.m., Karen, where have you been?" Olga scolded her as she glided through the door.

"I was out on a date."

Porter walked into the room as Olga continued. "You should have called us to say you would miss supper."

Karen mood soured. "Sorry, Olga, but I was having a good time, and I didn't want to ruin it by saying I had to call you. I'm 17 and can make my own decisions now."

"Look. You have been acting very un-Christian over the past few months. We are extremely worried about you," Olga's voice trembled as she glanced at Porter. "As your parents, we still have a say in your actions."

Karen shook her head, a dismissive scoff escaping her lips. "Don't confuse my freedom to do what I want with being a good Christian. I feel stifled here, like I'm trapped in a cage. You don't even care about my date, do you, Olga?"

Her lips mashed together in a hard line. "You're grounded for a week."

Karen smiled. "Sorry, but the Fall Recital is on Saturday night. You can't ground me because I have an important duet to perform. Besides, you're not my mother."

"There you go again. Do I need to call your grandfather?"

"I'll save you the trouble and just stay there tonight," she snapped, storming out the front door.

Chapter 1

A chill ran through her body as she and John waited in line at the Rockford Theatre. They were taking advantage of a buy-one, get-one-free promotion for Valentine's Day. Karen wished she had chosen a warmer outfit; a plaid skirt and a sweater underneath her winter jacket were not enough. *Form over function*, she thought, as the north wind reminded her that winter was still in charge of Rockford. She grabbed John's arm and huddled closer to stay warm.

Linda Jenkins, last year's homecoming princess, drew John's gaze as she swept past with her friends. Dressed impeccably in an elegant fur princess coat and striking red heels, she showcased her long, sculpted legs and beautiful shoulder-length brunette hair. She caught John's eye, flashing him a confident smile before gliding away. Karen glanced at John, her smile faltering, and retracted her arm.

"Do you like her?" Karen snipped, staring into John's eyes.

"No, Karen, no… of course not," he stammered.

"Then why did you stare at her?" she asked. Her hazel eyes burned into his like a sharp dagger.

"I've never seen her before," he said, looking away.

Karen's eyes narrowed as she continued her laser-focused stare. He looked into her eyes, revealing the truth.

Karen crossed her arms and muttered, "Humph."

The line began to move as the ticket booth opened. While their lively classmates from Rockford West laughed and joked, John and Karen stood there, looking around at everything but each other, as they shuffled to the front of the line.

"Do you want some popcorn and a soda?" John asked after they got inside.

"No," she snapped.

"Okay."

They took their seats as the theater started to fill up. "This is the fourth Hitchcock movie I've been to," John said. "I really liked Dial M for Murder. I hope this one is as good." Karen stared straight ahead, her arms crossed.

She glared as Linda and her friends walked in and took their seats. She watched John out of the corner of her eye as he tried not to look at them.

"Maybe you'd rather sit with *her*, John?" she quipped.

North by Northwest was a gripping thriller.

"I liked the ending," Karen said as they walked back to his car. "How romantic that Thornhill saves her from the fall at Mount Rushmore."

Chapter 1

"For me, the best part was when Thornhill was nearly killed in the middle of nowhere by a person in a plane," John gushed, his eyes bright with the memory. He swung open the car door for Karen, then slid into the driver's seat. Their gazes locked, holding for several breathless seconds.

"Do you love me, John?" Karen demanded. "I mean, do you *really* love me?"

"Karen, of course, I love you," he said, his blue eyes never leaving hers. She could see the sincerity shining through the glow of the car's interior lights. Karen felt a warm feeling wash over her.

"Then start this car so I can warm up, please," she smiled.

John chuckled as he turned the key. He grabbed her hand as they started driving home.

A few minutes later, after hearing the shocking news about the Buddy Holly crash in Iowa on the radio, he parked the car and turned off the engine.

"Thank you for taking me out on Valentine's Day, John," she said, smiling and leaning toward him. He gently pressed his lips to hers, savoring the softness. Their tongues began to intertwine. Their breathing quickened as she reached behind his neck to pull him closer. His hand wandered beneath her skirt, resting on her nyloned knee, as their passion continued to grow.

She thought, *I can't come on too strong with them watching*, so she pulled away and smiled. They exchanged a glance for a few moments before he walked around to open the passenger door, offering his hand as she got out of the car.

She gave him a quick peck and said, "Goodnight, John," then headed toward the front door. She could feel him watching her as she walked away.

"Northwestern and Augustana are two of the best universities in the country, Karen," her dad suggested. "Besides, both schools are only a couple of hours away from Rockford. You can come home here on weekends," he smiled.

"But with my grades, I can get accepted to many different schools, like Stanford, Columbia, Penn State, and Concordia. All of my friends are applying to schools nationwide."

"Yes, but they are quite a distance from Rockford. Stanford is on the West Coast, while Penn State and Columbia are in the Northeast. I think you'd like it better in the Midwest."

Chapter 1

Karen sighed. "Well, it wouldn't hurt to apply to these schools and see if I get accepted. I mean, why not?"

Georgene and Karen sat in a booth at The Last Straw, watching the flashing red lights and sirens echo through the restaurant. Employees hurried to bring the Fire Engine Special, a unique malt made just for birthday celebrants, to an excited 10-year-old boy. As the lights and sirens faded, the restaurant came alive with the sounds of *Happy Birthday*.

"Why didn't we ever do this for our birthdays, Karen?" Georgene asked once things had calmed down. "I think about that every time I come in here. The Fire Engine Special is worth it."

"It's the best part of coming here," Karen agreed, taking a drag from her cigarette. "Have you heard back from any of the schools yet?"

"Only one. I've been accepted to Northwestern," Georgene said, shrugging her shoulders.

"Well, that's a start!" Karen said. "At least you have something to fall back on."

"Northwestern accepts everybody, Karen," Georgene said matter-of-factly. "Last week, you got your acceptance letter, too. Did you get any other acceptance letters?"

"Yeah, Concordia College in Minnesota. My grandpa wants me to go there; it's a Lutheran college."

"What did you write about in your essay for Columbia University?" Georgene asked.

"I just summarized my accomplishments," Karen said. "My work with preschoolers at my Sunday school class and my tenure as the first viola in the school orchestra for two years. I also dedicated a paragraph to my volunteer efforts, tutoring students struggling academically, too."

"Smart," Georgene said, sipping her chocolate malt. "Well, it's still early for both of us. Do you still want to be roommates if we get into Columbia together?"

"Of course! Just imagine… New York City!" Karen said. "Times Square! Shopping on Fifth Avenue! Going to a Broadway show!"

Georgene added, "The Statue of Liberty, New York-style pizza, and Central Park. And don't forget about all the museums."

"I don't know how people go to school there. There are so many fun things to do!" They grinned at each other, their thoughts wandering to the future.

Chapter 1

"When did Sherman's March to the Sea take place?" her dad asked. Outside, the fierce afternoon snowstorm guaranteed they'd have a snow day tomorrow.

"From November to December 1864," Karen responded.

"Correct. And what was the date of the South's surrender to the Union?"

"April 9, 1865."

"Where?"

"At the Appomattox Court House in Virginia."

"Right again. How do you feel about this?" he asked.

"Good, I've been tutoring students in my class, too," Karen replied.

He closed the American History book. "Karen, I want to talk to you about the three of us."

"Okay," Karen replied, with a trace of skepticism in her voice.

"Your mother and I are eager to work through the issues in our relationship with you. For years, we have been saddened by the misunderstandings between us. We love you very much and care deeply for you. Our hope is to restore the bond we once shared and guide you back onto a more Christian path."

"You mean, before you guys told me I was adopted," Karen said.

Porter's shoulders slumped, and his eyes filled with a poignant blend of nostalgia and sorrow. His voice quivered as he addressed Karen. "Years ago, you were such a wonderful daughter. I still remember those evenings when you and your mother would play the piano after supper. The melodies would fill our home with warmth and joy, creating memories that linger with us today. But lately, it feels like you're drifting further away from God and from us. I can't help but worry about you every time you leave the house."

"Well, you guys need to stop being so demanding," Karen replied. "I have a lot of responsibilities with school and orchestra, and I have a boyfriend."

"Your mother and I came up with an idea. After supper, we want you to start taking piano lessons with her again."

"Why?"

"It would allow you and her to share something you both love," he said. "It's just for a few minutes each night."

Karen sighed. "I don't have time for this. It's nonsense."

"It would mean a lot to us if you tried. We spoke with your grandfather, and he agrees with us."

Karen closed her eyes and nodded her head with a sigh. "Fine. I'll do it."

Chapter 1

After supper that night, Karen and Olga settled at the piano, the keys beckoning after four silent years. Olga's eyes sparkled with joy as she prepared to guide her former student. Just as they had long ago, their fingers danced through the scales, the familiar patterns flowing effortlessly. Then, together, they explored the melodies from the Lutheran Hymnal. Over the years, Karen had blossomed into an exceptional musician, each note ringing with precision and depth.

After 30 minutes, Karen asked, "Can we practice something besides hymns tomorrow?"

"Of course, dear."

"I really need to study now."

"Yes, and thank you, Karen," Olga replied. She watched as her daughter ran off to her room. Her heart soared with a new hope.

The next day, she braved the stubborn snowstorm, driving through the swirling flakes to visit Guzzardo's. She returned laden with sheet music for Karen. Every night after supper, Karen and Olga created duets from the piano, their shared language transforming their relationship. The icy distance that once separated them started to dissolve with each passing night. Porter, ever supportive, even relegated himself to dish duty in the kitchen.

A couple of weeks later, Karen arrived home two hours after supper. As she walked in, Olga confronted her.

"Where were you today? You missed supper and piano practice," Olga demanded.

"I was studying at Georgene's house for Friday's chemistry test," Karen said. "I'm struggling with the periodic table elements. Georgene's mother invited me to stay for supper."

"You should have called and told me."

"What is more important—doing well in my schoolwork or making you happy by playing piano? You want me to do well in college, right?"

"Yes, but this is disrespectful of my time, Karen."

"Yes, Mother!" she sneered, dropping into an exaggerated curtsy. With a defiant toss of her head, she marched to her room, the door slamming shut behind her.

The following night after supper, Olga said, "Porter, would you clean the table while Karen and I play piano, please?"

Karen sighed. "I can't tonight. I need to study for my chemistry test on Friday."

"Just for a few minutes, Karen."

Chapter 1

"I said no!" Karen yelled.

"Playing piano will help relieve some of the stress you are under," Olga suggested.

"No, playing piano is something you want to do. I don't have time tonight."

"No, you are going to play piano with me. It's not a request."

The two women locked eyes, a tense silence hanging between them. Taking a deep breath, Karen marched to her room, grabbing her textbooks and viola. Without a word, she swept past Olga and Porter, wrenching open the front door and slamming it shut behind her.

Olga let out a heavy sigh. The piano lessons were yet another failed attempt to bring her back into the fold. She needed a new approach before Karen left for college in the fall.

For years, Karen had longed for a life full of new experiences, dreaming of a future in a busy city far from Rockford. In the spring, she received acceptance letters from four schools: Stanford, Columbia,

Concordia, and Augustana. Columbia was her top choice. Georgene had also been accepted, and they were excited to attend school together in New York. However, deep down, she knew her dad and grandfather didn't want her to live far away, even if it was with Georgene. After weighing her options, she decided that Concordia College in Minnesota was the best choice for her. It wasn't too far from home, but far enough for her to feel independent. But would the family accept her decision?

"Those poor people," Olga said, taking a bite of mashed potatoes.

"We should keep them in our prayers tonight," Grandpa said, looking at Grandma. "Could you please pass the green-bean casserole, dear?"

Porter added, "The news dubbed it the Palm Sunday Nor'easter. It dumped 35 inches of snow in Boston over four days, then the temperatures dropped well below zero."

"Whoa," Karen exclaimed.

"I heard that 40 people have died due to roof cave-ins and lack of heat. Many froze because they rely on gas to heat their homes," Olga said.

There was a lull in the conversation. Karen grabbed the moment.

Chapter 1

"After careful consideration, I've decided to attend Concordia College in Moorhead, Minnesota, this fall."

Her grandfather was pleased. "Praise the Lord. I'm glad you chose to attend Concordia College. It's a quality Lutheran school. But why not Augustana College? It is also an excellent Lutheran school, and it's very close."

Karen hesitated about what to say. "Grandpa, Augustana just didn't feel like the right fit."

"Well, at least you're not heading to the East Coast with all those big snowstorms," Olga added.

"You and your father went to Augustana a month ago, but never visited Concordia College," her grandpa asked. "How do you know you'll like it there? Also, the winters are significantly colder and have more snowfall."

"I don't know. I want to go there."

"Maybe before you decide, we should drive up there and take a campus tour," Olga suggested. "You might not like the brutal winters."

She glared at Olga. "I've decided to attend Concordia this fall. Do you have a problem with that?"

Olga's gaze swept across the table, settling on her daughter. "Yes, I do. You won't be able to come home on weekends to do laundry or spend time with your friends," she explained.

"You mean spend time with you? All my friends will be at school," Karen interjected. "Why don't you want me to go there?"

Olga begged the table for support with her eyes.

"Karen, the fifth commandment is to honor your mother and father," her grandfather said, "and at this table, you will show some respect for your elders."

"Yes, sir," Karen replied.

"Your mother makes a good point. It would be helpful for you to plan a trip to Moorhead to visit the school, learn about the winters, and get a feel for their programs. Also, drive around to see how much you like the city. Only then should you decide."

"Fine, I'll contact them and schedule a tour through the admissions office." Karen muttered, the words laced with resignation."

"Praise the Lord."

Early one Saturday morning, Karen and Porter began their eight-hour trek to Moorhead. Karen engineered the trip for a weekend when Olga's church duties precluded her involvement. Concordia College, much like Augustana, boasted a long-held tradition of excellence, ranking among the nation's premier

Chapter 1

Lutheran institutions. Its campus buzzed with a vibrant cultural tapestry, hosting students from over 100 nations. Moorhead, with its trendy vibe, attracted visitors with a variety of cultural and outdoor activities during the summer. Karen found herself captivated by the locals' friendliness and openness, a quality referred to as "Minnesota nice."

During the return journey, Karen's passion for the school and city soared. Initially drawn to Concordia by its distance from her family, she now embraced it as the ideal launchpad for her college journey.

Chapter 2

Howard grabbed Nellie's udders (one of their seven heifers) and began squeezing her milk into a bucket. Their new transistor radio was replaying highlights of President Eisenhower's inauguration speech, in which he promised an era of global peace and international cooperation in the face of communism.

Since the war's end, the United States had spearheaded a constant flow of exciting new technologies and advancements. But President Eisenhower understood the need for ethics and principles in these changing times. Howard particularly liked the quote, "A people that value its privileges above its principles soon loses both." He believed in Ike. After all, he had been the General in charge of D-Day and was a charismatic leader.

After tending to the pigs, heifers, and chickens, gathering the eggs, and scrubbing the barn, Howard's nostrils caught the fragrance of bacon and eggs wafting from the house. As the sky lightened with dawn's first hues, his stomach clamored for breakfast. Trudging towards the house, the crisp morning air bit at his cheeks as he balanced a basket of eggs and a metal bucket of milk, clanking against his leg. He mentally reviewed a few more words for his spelling test. *Consequence C-o-n-s-e-q-u-a-n-c-e. No, is that right?*

He hauled the eggs and milk into the kitchen and laid them down with a thud. longing for the bacon by the stove.

"Morning, Mom," he said, walking over to the stove. The pancake batter in the cast-iron skillet sizzled as he looked on.

"Good morning, dear. Go get ready for school now, breakfast will be ready in a few minutes."

He took a quick shower, threw on his favorite fleece sweater and some jeans over his long johns, and pinned his Marshal Dillon badge above his heart. He pointed two finger guns at the mirror and shouted, "Pow, pow!" before heading back to the kitchen.

His father peeked from behind the newspaper as he sat down. "Did you finish all your chores, Howard?"

"Yes, sir. Nellie produced more milk this morning, and she looks better."

"Good. The part arrived at Abraham's yesterday for the International, so I will start repairing the PTO shaft today. When you get done with school, would you help me?"

Chapter 2

"Yes, of course! Can you show me how it works, too?"

"Yes, if there is time before supper."

"Maybe I can work the International this season? Dick's dad lets him plow the fields."

"Will see."

Howard was starving, but he waited for his mother to sit down and his father to fold the St. Paul Pioneer Press. He licked his lips and gazed at the bacon, savoring its rich, savory aroma. Bacon was rare during the week; it was usually reserved for Sunday dinner after church.

Like his parents, he folded his hands and recited, "Come Lord Jesus, be our guest. Let these gifts to us be blessed. Amen."

As Howard reached for the bacon and took a bite, he checked the clock. He had about twenty minutes before he needed to leave for school.

His mother looked at him. "Can you spell 'fortune'?"

"F-o-r-t-u-n-e," he replied.

"Don't talk with your mouth full," his mom ordered.

He swallowed his food and then repeated the spelling.

"Good, spell anguish," she replied.

"A-n-g-w-i-s-h."

"No, try again."

"Mom, I'm trying to eat!" he complained, but she just stared at him, waiting for a response.

"Is it a-n-g-u-i-s-h?" he replied.

"Correct. Do you feel ready for the test?" she asked while his dad took a bite of his eggs and continued reading the newspaper.

"Dick and I were quizzing each other last night. Some of the words are tricky to spell because they don't sound like they're spelled."

"Being a skilled speller matters. Misspellings will undermine the credibility of your writing, causing readers to question the validity of your content. Mrs. Donaldson demands a higher level of spelling accuracy than I did at the schoolhouse."

"She makes everyone spell the words, even the little kids."

"Good. Never too early to learn to spell."

Layering up is key to staying warm against the harsh Minnesota wind. You need three layers: long johns right against your skin, a cozy fleece layer, and a solid outer shell. Howard slipped on his snow boots and

Chapter 2

grabbed his coat, hat, mittens, and scarf. He tossed his backpack over his coat and shouted, "Bye!"

Outside, his trusty Harold Racer was parked next to the house, with a light dusting of snow from the night before. He grabbed the sled and made his way to the road. Up ahead, Dick was already waiting.

"Hey, Dick!" Howard shouted, casting a jealous glance at Dick's pride and joy—a brand-new fire-engine-red Silver Streak sled that he'd received for Christmas just a couple of weeks ago. Dick would not allow anyone to ride it, let alone even touch it!

"You ready for the test?" Dick asked as they started walking towards the schoolhouse.

"Not really," Howard sighed. "What did you think of last night's episode?"

"I liked it. I wasn't sure how Marshal Dillon would get out of that one."

Howard thought back to Christmas Day. The best gift he'd been given this year came in a small envelope. Inside was a card with the Gunsmoke logo at the top. On the right side, there was a picture of Marshal Dillon pointing his gun, and on the left side, a heavy metal badge that read, "Matt Dillon, U.S. Marshal." It looked exactly like his badge from the show.

"Well, go ahead and try it on!" his mother had said as Howard admired the badge. He ripped the badge off the card, hurried to the bathroom, and slipped the badge through his shirt.

"Wow," he exclaimed, gazing at his reflection. Then he returned to the living room and gave his mother a big hug.

"Thanks, Mom! This is the best gift ever!"

Howard had worn the badge every day since Christmas. He tapped his jacket to make sure it was still there.

Up ahead, kids hurled down Sugarloaf Pass, the mile-long downhill stretch leading to the schoolhouse. They maneuvered their rattling sleds through the twists and turns, masters of the ice-packed dirt road.

Howard counted down 30 seconds and got a running start before hopping on. He raced along the winding gravel road, clocking fifteen miles per hour on the straightaways. "Behind you!" he yelled, overtaking the younger girl who had left 30 seconds before him. At the bottom, a throng of kids stared as sleds whizzed past, their collective memory reliving their adrenaline rush. It was the absolute highlight of every school day.

Howard kept looking for more gifts under the Christmas tree. Compared to last year, when he got the

Chapter 2

Marshal Dillon badge, he didn't get much this year—a couple of Sunday shirts, some notebooks for school, and a little cash. *Well, at 14, maybe I'm too old for Christmas gifts*, he thought.

"Are you going to eat your pie?" his mother asked, looking at his half-eaten blueberry pie sitting next to the sofa.

"I'm savoring it, Mom," Howard replied. Mom made a blueberry pie every Christmas and Easter; every bite tasted like heaven.

His dad rested his pipe, and the warm smell of tobacco drifted through the air. With a smile, he rose from his cherished orange armchair—the off-limits space reserved for him alone. He strolled into the kitchen, pausing to stare at the clear night sky.

"You know, I think we left the heater on in the barn," his dad said as he walked back into the living room. "We need to go outside and turn it off." Turning off the heater required two people: one at the thermostat and the other at the heater itself. His dad had bought the heater when they'd first got electricity on the farm five years ago, and it'd been a game changer for working over the winter months.

Howard thought for a moment. "You're right. After I got back from town, you were already inside," Howard sighed. It was below 0 °F tonight.

"Well, let's go," his dad motioned for him to stand up.

"I'll clean up the mess here," his mom said.

Bundled in overcoats and boots, Howard and his dad battled the fierce north wind. Howard wrenched open the barn door, unleashing a blast of warm air into the frigid night. Inside, his dad secured the door, cutting off the chill with a solid bang.

Howard searched for the light switch on the side of the barn. After flipping it on, he glanced back at his dad and said, "I'll run up to the heater."

As he turned, he froze in his tracks. Nestled comfortably in the heart of the barn was a gleaming 1957 Ford tractor, its vibrant red and white paint was shining like a freshly minted dime. The unmistakable scent of new machinery—a mix of metal and fresh oil—filled the barn.

"Oh, wow! Dad, did you get a new tractor?" Howard asked, looking back at his dad. "It wasn't here this afternoon."

"It just got delivered," his dad replied, grinning. "Tom Heffernan came out here personally to deliver it."

"I didn't know Tom was here?"

"You and your mother had gone into town because she needed some French-fried potatoes before the Red Owl closed."

Chapter 2

Howard climbed onto the seat. It featured a five-speed transmission with a reverse gear. These new Ford tractors were real workhorses. Designed for farms of all sizes, they were the most technologically advanced in the world. Just then, the barn door opened, and his mom walked in.

"What do you think?" his dad asked Howard.

"It's small, but these Ford tractors can do almost anything. I've read about these in Ag Monthly."

"It's yours," his dad said with a smile as he wrapped his arm around his wife.

"Wait?" Howard said, "You're giving *me* this tractor?"

"Yes."

Howard pushed down the clutch and turned the key, waking the Ford up with a roar. His mom and dad walked around their new toy, admiring the red and white paint job. Howard hopped off the tractor and took a good look at the engine.

"Did you get any implements to go with it?" Howard asked as he reached over and turned off the engine.

"Tom included a tiller and a blade at no cost, but you'll need to wait until March for them to arrive. The reading material he provided includes a catalog with over 40 implements."

Chapter 2

"What do you say to your father?" his mom asked.

"Thanks, Dad!" came the heartfelt reply.

"And that's not all. Starting next season, you will assume responsibility for corn production in the back 40. You will use this tractor to work the field. You need to prepare the field, order and plant the seeds, and maintain a schedule for watering, weeding, and fertilizing during the school year. In the fall, we will use the International for harvesting. You need to browse the implements catalog and determine which attachments you need for your field. We will visit Tom in a couple of days and place your order. Would you like to take on this big responsibility, Howard?"

"Yes, oh yes! Thank you!" Howard said, grinning from ear to ear.

Howard settled into the passenger seat of the black 1957 Ford Fairlane 500. His dad had bought the car last November, part of a package deal that included his Ford tractor. Despite his aversion to black cars—he had grumbled, "It highlights the dust too clearly"—Tom Heffernan had presented him with an irresistible offer for both, sweetening the deal with a significant price reduction.

In January, they drove the new car off the lot at Tom Hefferman's Ford dealership, leaving their old 1955 Ford behind. Howard could still make out that new car scent, even though it was nine months ago. It was their first luxury car, boasting a five-speed automatic transmission and a powerful 500cc engine. When his dad settled into the driver's seat, Howard felt his surge of pride; it was a testament to their successful 1956 season.

His dad eased out of the driveway and sped down the dirt road toward Lake City. Dust billowed behind them, a consequence of a week-long drought. He tuned the radio to WCCO, where Cedric Adams continued to dissect the standoff in Little Rock involving the nine Black students at Central High School, known as the "Little Rock Nine." President Eisenhower had deployed the National Guard to facilitate integration.

They descended Sugarloaf Pass and swept past the old schoolhouse he had attended for ten years. As they flew by, he glanced at Mrs. Donaldson, instructing the students. As the dirt road transitioned to blacktop, the 500cc engine surged to life. His dad loved the power of his new toy.

Howard had spent the entire night in bed rehearsing for this moment. He took a deep breath. "Dad, now that I'm 15, I would like to get my driver's license. Many kids my age already have theirs, and I want one too. Plus, if I could drive myself to school, it would save you the trouble of taking me to the bus stop every day. This would free up your time."

"And what will you drive if you get your license?"

"I can drive the '52 Ford."

"No," his dad said, shaking his head. "That car hasn't run in years; we use it for spare parts now. I don't want to spend money fixing it."

"Dick and I checked out the car the other day. It needs a new battery, a master cylinder, a radiator, and some tires. I've been saving up my allowance to buy the parts at Abraham's. If Dick and I can get it running, would you let me get my license and drive it?"

"Well, Howard, I'm not sure. You haven't shown much responsibility for the corn in the back 40. Last Christmas, I gave you the Ford tractor and assigned you the responsibility for half the farm, but you've been quite lax in maintaining the field this season. Remember, you agreed to manage the back 40, even during the school year."

Howard sighed. *It always comes back to the farm*, he thought.

His dad continued. "I checked out your field yesterday. I saw a lot of weeds, plus the husks are showing signs of dehydration. I watered the field for you yesterday, but you need to handle plowing the weeds. It needs to be done today, right after school."

"But Dick and I were going to go out with our friends to the A&W drive-in after school! There is a girl named Mary who will be there."

"Well, if I pick you up from school, you can finish it before supper. Then you can go out with your friends."

"I can't do that. Dad, I'll take care of it this weekend."

"The weeds need to be tended today, not on Saturday."

They sat quietly for a few seconds. Howard crossed his arms. "Fine. Pick me up from school."

"Good. And I'll consider the '52 Ford once you show more responsibility for your duties on the farm."

Howard shook his head. "The farm… the farm… It's always the farm," he mumbled to himself.

They pulled up to the bus stop. "Have a good day at school, Howard. I'll see you at 2:30."

Without saying a word, Howard grabbed his books and slammed the door behind him.

"Crescent wrench," Dick's voice echoed from beneath the '52 Ford. Howard leaned down, sliding the tool to

Chapter 2

his best friend. Paul Anka's *My Hometown* drifted from the radio. Within seconds, Dick wheeled out from under the car on the creeper.

"Okay, done. You can start putting the new oil in," he said as he stood up.

Howard pierced the oil spout into the metal can and poured it into the crankcase.

"I'm not sure I want to stay here, Dick. I want to explore the world. I want to see what's out there. There's so much more than Lake City and this farm."

"Yeah, you've talked about that for a while now. What would you do?"

"I don't know yet."

"How does your dad feel about that?" Dick asked. "My parents are thinking about retirement in a few years. If I choose to go to college, I have brothers who can take over the farm. But since you're an only child... well, that's tough."

"I know," Howard muttered.

"Have you talked to your career counselor yet? As seniors, we have to decide on our post-graduation plans. Maybe she can give you some ideas? I'm considering seminary school."

"You? A pastor?" A smirk played on his lips.

"It's one suggestion she gave me," Dick said, raising his voice slightly. "I think you should explore some options for your future, too. Talk to your career counselor. If I were you, I would go to college and see how you feel about farming after graduation. You might change your mind and realize that country life isn't so bad after all." Dick stretched out his arms. "Wouldn't you miss stepping in cow pies and hearing roosters crowing at 5 a.m. every morning?" he asked, giving Howard a friendly slap on the back.

Howard added, "Yeah, and tractors that break down in the middle of a field and working from sunrise to sunset." He opened another can of motor oil.

Dick shifted the conversation. "So, we get to vote in our first election this November. Who do you support?"

"I like the guy from Massachusetts, Senator Kennedy. He's young and exciting, and I believe he would do a better job than Nixon," Howard replied. "There are so many changes happening in the world right now, and I feel he's the right man for the job. Nixon represents the past, while Kennedy is the future."

"Yeah, I agree with you, Howard. Well said."

Evelyn waved at the mailman's Jeep from the garden as he made his weekly delivery. After gathering the last of

Chapter 2

the spring peas, she trudged towards the muddy road to retrieve the mail. By March, the snow had mostly melted, leaving everything a muddy mess.

The mail contained two bills and a letter from her sister, Florence. There was also a letter addressed to Howard from the School of Agriculture at the University of Minnesota in St. Paul.

She walked to the house and placed Howard's letter on the kitchen table. Staring at it, she contemplated what it meant for their lives. Howard was becoming more distant every month. Although he kept up with his farming chores, his heart didn't seem to be in it. He spent most of his time in Lake City with his friends. He came home for supper at six and then studied until bedtime. His father kept reminding him that planting season was approaching and that he should start ordering seeds and getting the back 40 ready for the season. The dread of responsibility for another growing season was clear on Howard's face.

The two men in her life entered the house just as she finished cooking supper. Her husband arrived first from the barn, where he had been preparing the tiller and seeder attachments on Howard's Ford tractor for the upcoming season.

They embraced. "A letter arrived from the University of Minnesota," she said, indicating the envelope beside Howard's plate on the kitchen table.

"Oh, I see," he responded, then headed off to clean up for supper. He had always struggled to express his emotions in the moment.

She called after him. "Will you make him the offer we talked about if he is accepted?" He didn't respond.

A minute later, Howard's '52 Ford pulled into the driveway. He rushed into the house, kissed her on the cheek, and sat down at the table at 6 p.m. sharp. Evelyn smiled as his gaze fixed on the letter, then snapped up to her.

"It came today," she replied. He picked it up and stared at the words, "Official Correspondence."

His dad entered and took a seat as she was setting the food on the table. "Well, are you going to open it or just stare at it?" he asked with a grin.

Howard ripped open the envelope and scanned its contents.

"Well…?" his mother asked.

Howard looked at her with a mix of disbelief and joy lighting up his eyes. "I've been accepted!" he exclaimed. "I can't believe it! I'm actually in!"

"I'm so happy for you, dear. When do your classes begin?" she asked, eager to know more about this new chapter in his life.

"It says here Monday, August 23rd," he said, searching for more details. "I will be assigned a dorm

Chapter 2

room on Friday, August 13th, and I must report for class registration on Monday, August 16th. Wow, that's only five months away."

"It is also right in the middle of the season," his dad added. "Who is going to finish up the back 40 this year?"

"I guess you are, Dad."

His dad clenched a roll and tore into it sharply. No one spoke. The quiet thickened as Howard dished up his plate.

"I am very proud of you, son," his mother said, looking at his father.

"I've given this a lot of thought," his dad finally said. "You've shown that you know how to run the farm, but you need more ambition to make it thrive. I want you to learn these new techniques and advancements in farming, but I want to see more ambition from you if I decide to give you this farm one day." He looked Howard in the eye. "With that said, I've decided to pay for your education."

"Really?"

His dad smiled and said, "For years, I've read about all the advancements in the farming industry, and I fully support you learning these new agricultural techniques. And the University of Minnesota is one of the top agricultural schools in the country. From my perspective, your education is an investment in the future of this farm."

"Great! Now I don't have to apply for student loans."

"Here is my plan: This year, you will be responsible for the back 40 during the planting and growing seasons. I will take over responsibilities in August before the harvest season."

He continued. "For the next four years at school, over your Christmas break and summer vacations from school, I expect you to help me on the farm. Additionally, I need you to be home on weekends during both the harvest and planting seasons," he said. "As you learn new ideas and advancements we can use on the farm, we can begin implementing them here."

"Okay, I guess."

"What do you mean, 'I guess'?"

"It's a significant commitment. Every Christmas and all summer? And I have to come home on weekends during planting and harvest seasons, too? What about study time for my exams?"

"Son, this farm is your future. You're needed here, too. When you head off to school, I'll get the Anderson boy to help me during the week."

His excitement crumbled. Four years of divided commitment? It loomed like a prison sentence, but it outweighed the crushing burden of student loan debt.

Chapter 2

"Okay," he muttered, a wave of resignation washing over him. "I'll do it."

"Good choice, son. I'm really proud of you for getting into the U of M."

Chapter 3

"Yes, Grandpa, everything is okay," Karen said.

"The weatherman said the brunt of the snowstorm is going right through Moorhead," he said. "How much snow have you received so far?"

"It's a lot," she said, gazing out the windows of the Social Hub. "I've never seen so much snow! The news said 18 inches had already fallen. They've announced that the college will be closed on Monday because the snowstorm is expected to last through the night."

"Thank God. You don't need to be out in that," he replied, sounding relieved.

"Grandpa, since everything on campus is connected, I don't need to be outside for long. It's just 30 steps from Livedalen Hall to the Hub, and I'm back inside."

"Wow, that's interesting. So, it's mostly an indoor campus, then? That makes sense in such a cold part of Minnesota. How is your roommate?"

"She's fantastic! She decided to transfer to UND – Fargo next year. They have a better medical program than Concordia College."

"How exciting for her! Have you decided on a major yet?"

"Nope, not yet. But it's only the first quarter, so that'll happen, Grandpa. The main thing that bugs me is the rules. They're very strict with dress codes and curfew hours—especially for women."

"Like I told you before, those are there for your protection, Karen," he said as he cleared his throat. "Well, I'm glad you called. I have a request."

"Of course, Grandpa. What is it?"

"Would you please call your mother?" he asked.

"Why?" Karen asked.

"Because she's worried about you being in such a brutal snowstorm," he said. "I want you to call her right away. You haven't called your parents since you moved to Moorhead two months ago."

"Okay, Grandpa. I'll call her now."

"Praise God. Okay, I'll pray for you tonight."

"Bye, Grandpa," Karen said and hung up the phone.

Karen stared out the window at the falling snow. She really didn't want to talk to her mom, but they were paying for her to go to college. Maybe she could talk about herself. She picked up the phone, dialed the number, and inserted three dollars' worth of quarters.

Porter answered the phone.

Chapter 3

"Hi Dad!" Karen replied, relieved that Olga hadn't answered the phone first.

"Hi Karen! It's great to hear from you. How is Concordia?"

"It's cold. Grandpa asked me to call you guys."

"Okay," he replied, his voice fading. "Olga! Karen's on the phone," he shouted. "The weatherman said there was a massive snowstorm in the Fargo/Moorhead area. How are you doing?"

"Oh, I'm fine. Big, fluffy flakes of snow have been coming down for hours. They canceled school tomorrow."

"How are your classes?" he asked.

"They're easy. Remember, I'm only a freshman."

"Have you been enjoying dorm life?"

"I have! My roommate is wonderful, and I made some friends here in the dorm. It's fun!"

Karen heard Olga talking to Porter in the background. "Your mother asked if you played the viola or piano at church since starting school."

"No, I haven't played viola or piano yet, but I have been attending church every Sunday morning. There is a nice Lutheran church right here on campus," she replied. "The snow wasn't so bad this morning, so they didn't cancel church."

Olga grabbed the phone. "Honey, you should tell them you were the first viola in the high school orchestra and also play piano. I'm sure they'll find a way for you to contribute to the service. You're too talented to let that go to waste."

"Sure, okay. I will ask them," she replied, shaking her head.

"I miss you. When are you coming home? Will you be home here for Thanksgiving?"

"I won't, but winter break starts in mid-December, so I'll take the bus to Rockford for Christmas, okay?"

"What day is it?" Olga eagerly asked.

"I don't know yet, but I will let Grandpa know. We talk every Sunday night."

"Well, let us know, too! After all, we are your parents."

"Okay, Mom," Karen said with a sigh. "I have to go now. Bye!" She hung up the receiver, rolling her eyes.

By the end of the Fall quarter, every freshman at Concordia was required to select two or three potential majors. Karen was mainly interested in education, but lately, her roommate has been teaching her the impact of diet on health. As a med student, she was careful about what she ate and practiced a healthy lifestyle. Karen found this idea intriguing.

She asked some of her dormmates about this field one day while talking in the Social Hub.

"It's a fascinating field," someone replied. "I took Introduction to Nutrition as a freshman. Did you know eating food from a dented can is unsafe?"

"Why?" Karen replied.

"A sharp dent could compromise the seal and let bacteria in the can," she replied.

"Gross."

"I went through that class, too," another responded. "We covered food preparation across various cultures, the science of how food impacts your body, and how dietary changes can positively affect your life. It was a good course."

She was sold. Karen signed up for the Introduction to Nutrition class for the winter quarter. She was surprised by how drinking eight glasses of water daily could have a significant impact on her health. After listening to her professor, she began making meaningful changes to her diet. She began to feel healthier, and her overall well-being improved.

On the bus ride back to Rockford in December, she hoped that her relationship with her family would improve over the holidays. *Maybe the time away will have helped them realize just how hovering they were*, she thought. She made a mental note to call Georgene and John to see if they are coming home for Christmas, too. They had so much to talk about! She also decided she wanted to become a Registered Dietitian.

Her parents welcomed her with warm, loving smiles at the vibrant bus station. There was no place on earth like Christmas in Rockford—the spirit of the season filled the air. The downtown area buzzed with excitement as joyful shoppers hurried from store to store, carrying colorful shopping bags. Each shop window sparkled with elaborate displays, showcasing shimmering green and red decorations that glistened under twinkling holiday lights. Each year, the window displays became more creative as they competed for the prestigious Best Window Display award in Rockford.

When they arrived home, the first thing she noticed was the Evergleam artificial Christmas tree in the corner, which always anchored the holiday celebration. Their favorite ornaments graced its branches, each one rekindling memories from past Christmases. The stockings dangled next to the tree, each one emblazoned with a name—Mom, Dad, and Karen—

with a soft glow of fairy lights dancing around them. Concordia's Christmas decorations dazzled her, but nothing compared to the feeling of spending Christmas in Rockford.

Karen caught up with her friend Georgene a few days before Christmas. They met at a bar in Wisconsin that they used to frequent on weekends during high school.

"Karen, you look fantastic!"

"How is Columbia, Georgene? Do you like living in New York?"

"Oh, yes, I love it! There are so many fun things to do!"

"Do you like the Columbia campus?"

"It's great! There are students from all over the world, Karen. My dorm roommate is from Portugal, and she's teaching me Portuguese. She made me something called *Bacalhau à Brás*, a traditional dish made with codfish, and it's delicious! We go to a Portuguese restaurant in Brooklyn once a week. She loves American culture, so we often do the touristy things. Last week, we visited Wall Street and watched the trading floor. It's amazing how much happens there. It's the center of commerce in the United States. We've visited the Statue of Liberty and the Empire State

Building, and we frequently visit Greenwich Village to check out the music scene. Hey, I almost forgot... there's a Greenwich Village musician from Minnesota named Bob Dylan, he's very popular. Have you heard of him?"

"No, I haven't."

"How is college life in... where is it again?" Georgene asked.

"Moorhead, Minnesota."

Georgene took a sip of her beer. "Yes, that's it. What are the fun things to do there?"

Karen looked down at her beer. "Well, not much. It snows a couple of times a week, so you are pretty much stuck on campus over the winter."

"Well, that's no fun! How long does the winter last?"

"The first snowstorm was a month after I arrived. They say it is supposed to last until April."

"Does it snow the entire school year? And there is nothing to do at all?"

Karen thought for a moment. "Well, study. I'm currently taking a nutrition course. Sometimes I go out drinking at the bars or go to house parties on the weekends with the girls from the dorm."

Georgene looked down on her. "Oh... fun!"

Chapter 3

This was not the Georgene whose laughter had echoed through Rockford West High School. This Georgene pulsated with a different energy, an unfamiliar confidence that jarred Karen, making her regret her choice of Concordia over Columbia. As she navigated the long stretch of highway back to Rockford, a chilling question **crystallized**: had their friendship ended?

The holiday was always a hectic two-day affair for the family. On Christmas Eve, they attended the afternoon service at Good Shepherd Lutheran Church in Rockford, Porter's home church. They typically attended Good Shepherd for Christmas and Easter services. Then, on Christmas morning, they traveled to Durand for her grandfather's Christmas service at Trinity Lutheran Church, their regular place of worship. After the service, they went back to her grandfather's house for Christmas dinner and gifts. The relaxing holiday dinner was a welcome break after two busy days.

"On the news, they said the snowfall will continue throughout the day, and they expect nearly five inches of accumulation," Porter said.

"Well, at least they'll have a white Christmas," Olga remarked, gazing outside the bay window at the dead grass and bare trees in the front yard.

"Do you think it will shut down the government?" Grandma asked.

Porter shook his head. "I doubt it. Washington, D.C. usually handles much more powerful snowstorms."

"God willing, they'll have the streets cleared in time for rush hour tomorrow morning," Grandpa said.

Karen took advantage of the lull in conversation. "I've made my decision about my major. I'm going to be a Registered Dietitian."

Olga asked, "What's that?"

"A dietitian tells patients the best foods for their dietary needs. It's the science of what you eat."

"Sounds like a fascinating field, Karen," her grandfather said. "What made you—"

"But what about your music?" Olga scoffed. "You're an excellent musician. You've never expressed interest in food or drink before. This is a ridiculous idea."

"Well, that's what I intend to do," Karen insisted.

Olga rolled her eyes and sighed.

"Can I be excused, please?" Karen asked, rising to her feet and gazing at her grandfather. He responded with a brief nod, and she went to sit in their guest bedroom.

A few minutes later, her grandfather walked in.

Chapter 3

"Your grandmother made a delicious pie. I thought you might like a slice," he asked.

"Thanks, Grandpa," she said as he set it down on the bedside table.

"She didn't mean what she said, Karen. She was just caught off guard because she always thought you'd be a musician. You are very musically gifted, Karen."

"Yeah, well, things change."

"I always thought you would become a schoolteacher. You did so well in the preschool class for years at church."

"No, I still like teaching. And a big part of being a dietitian is teaching others."

"Well, praise God you decided on a career path. I'm sure you will be the best dietitian in the whole world!" he replied.

Karen reached over and gave him a big hug. "Thanks, Grandpa! You're the best!"

Shortly after getting home from Morehead, she called John at Northwestern University to see if he was coming home for Christmas. Although they had broken up over the summer, they'd agreed to remain close friends. They made plans to meet on the 26th at The Last Straw.

Karen felt nervous about seeing John again. Even though it had only been four months, it felt like a lifetime had passed. She wore his favorite dress, the one that showed off her legs.

Arriving ahead of schedule, she noticed their first-date booth—the corner one by the window—was empty. As she sank into the familiar upholstery, her mind floated back to that unforgettable first encounter. His gentle, calming siren echoed within her as they perfected their duet for the Fall Recital. Fate had intervened that day, and their relationship flourished within the confines of The Last Straw. This was their special booth.

A few minutes later, he finally walked into the restaurant, overdressed in a suit and tie. It was the same suit he wore for their duet at their Fall Recital.

She stood up as he searched for her in the restaurant. He watched his eyes gravitate to her body as they met and hugged. "Karen, you look radiant! What have you been doing?"

"I started eating healthier. I'm going to be a dietitian."

They ordered two malts as they talked about all the changes in their lives. John had a girlfriend at Northwestern, and he'd brought her home to meet the family.

"She's nice like you, Karen."

"Where is she now?" Karen asked.

"I bought two tickets for The Nutcracker Suite at the Civic Opera House in Chicago tonight. Paula's getting ready at my parents' house right now."

"Wow, how exciting!" Karen said. "How come you never took me to the Opera House?" Karen smiled.

John's face lit up whenever he talked about Paula. His blue eyes sparkled with excitement as he recalled how they'd met in Music Theory class—a chance encounter when they'd sat next to each other during a lecture. He'd invited her to study, and they'd rendezvoused in the library that afternoon. Their conversations had flowed effortlessly, often drifting into passionate debates about the genius of Alfred Hitchcock or the finest classical composers.

"We had a special place we always met in the library," he told Karen. "It's so effortless with her, like destiny brought us together." A flicker of resentment sparked in Karen's eyes as he talked. She managed a polite grin, her jawline hardening beneath the forced pleasantness.

Chapter 3

Though Paula still lived with her parents in Wrigleyville during the week, they cherished Friday and Saturday nights in his dorm room at Northwestern. Karen could feel her anger bubble beneath the surface now.

"She sounds pretty, John," Karen said, forcing a smile. "Can I meet her?"

"Paula wanted to meet you, too. It felt a bit strange to me, but she kept insisting that she wanted to meet my little high school girlfriend, so I agreed. However, she and my mom went shopping at Ana Black's a couple of hours ago instead. She's still getting ready."

Little girlfriend? Karen took a sharp breath in. "Yeah, your mom and I used to go shopping there, too. It's her favorite store," Karen said. "This all seems so… sudden, John."

"She's perfect, Karen," John smiled, his voice warm and full of admiration. Years ago, he had given her this same look on their first date in this very booth.

This new girl had her claws in pretty deep. She forced another smile and said, "I'm so happy for you."

"So soon? We haven't seen you in months, and now you're heading back to Moorhead? We thought you were going to stay until New Year's Day?" Porter asked the next night at supper. "You've only been here for a week."

"Without any students, the school will be nice and quiet. Plus, there's nothing for me to do here. John and Georgene have their own lives. I just want to go home."

"This *is* your home," Olga retorted. "We miss you. We hoped to spend more time with you while you were here."

"Look," Karen snapped, her gaze unflinching. "I hated being here in high school, and I refuse to be here now. And no, I won't torture myself with more piano 'lessons' after supper."

"You will not talk to us that way. This is a Christian home, and we raised you with Christian values," Porter said.

Karen waved her finger at Porter. "You see! That's it. Right there. You two grew up in a different era, and you don't understand me at all. I am Christian; I'm just not the kind of Christian you want me to be. That's why I'm leaving early to go home."

"Alright, let's discuss this," Olga said, putting down her fork. "I've tried everything I can to be your mother."

Karen shrieked at Olga, her eyes blood red with fury. "Listen, you're not my mother," she said sharply, then whirled to face Porter. "And you're not my father. I have no idea who my parents are. What do they look

Chapter 3

like? Where do they live? Do I have any siblings? You both have the comfort of knowing your family, but for me, it's a complete mystery."

She turned back to Olga as the tears started to well up inside. "Imagine if you never knew your parents. How would your life be different?" She paused and wiped a tear from her eye. "Can you imagine what it felt like to be Baby Moses, abandoned by his parents, and drifting down the Nile. I can. It's a profound loneliness, Olga, being left behind by your parents in a big world. And because of you, I'll never know."

An uncomfortable silence gripped the table.

Karen stood up after a few seconds, staring Olga down. "Well, I guess you don't want to talk about it, huh? I'll stay at Grandpa's house tonight and catch a bus in the morning." In a blinding rage, she stormed back to her room, slamming her clothes into the suitcase.

Porter and Olga remained rooted at the dinner table as she finished packing and put on her coat. Olga wept openly, her sobs the only noise in the house. Porter lifted his gaze as she looked back.

"Don't go," he pleaded. "Please don't do this. We love you."

Karen hesitated momentarily, weighing her options. Remaining, she knew, would only ignite further conflict. "What's the use?" she muttered. Steeled by her decision, she snatched her suitcase, thrust open the front door, and yanked it shut behind her with a definitive crash. The trek to Grandpa's house would be long and cold, but it was better than the Arctic chill in that house.

The next morning, she gazed out the window of the Greyhound bus, watching the bright sun reflect off the snow-covered fields of Wisconsin. She heard a passenger snoring in the background, stopping whenever the bus hit a bump. Her eyes wandered back to page 144 of her Introduction to Nutrition textbook. *Was I too harsh on them? They're paying for college, after all...* Karen shook her head. *No, they need to understand. Being alone in the world is difficult. Without my birth parents, my childhood feels incomplete. They robbed me of that experience.*

As the band's somewhat off-key rendition of Elvis's *Can't Help Falling in Love* drifted across the packed dance floor, John had pulled her close, their lips meeting in a clumsy but tender kiss. Oh, how she'd wished that moment could freeze in time, shielding them forever from their looming adulthood. She remembered Georgene doing the splits in her prom

Chapter 3

dress, which had made Karen laugh so hard that she accidentally peed herself. Memories flooded back of all the Saturday night trips to Wisconsin when they would go to the bar and get utterly plastered. During their last orchestra trip to Milwaukee, the three of them had made a vow to stay friends forever.

Eight months ago, they had been her family. Now, as the bus sped along the treacherous, icy highway in Wisconsin, those days felt like a distant echo, dissolving further with each passing mile. The stinging cold and bleak landscape mirrored the widening chasm between her past and the stark solitude of her present. She sat rigidly, clutching her textbook, and wrestled her attention back to page 144.

"Well, we can meet right now, if you have time, Karen," the Concordia guidance counselor said. "With everyone on Christmas break, it is very quiet on campus."

"Great!" Karen replied as they walked back to her office.

"What's your last name, Karen?"

"Smith. Karen Ann Smith."

After digging through the file cabinet, the counselor sat down and studied her file.

"Good grades at an Illinois high school, along with involvement in orchestra, tutoring, and teaching Sunday school. You are a long way from home. Why did you choose Concordia?"

"I'm from a Lutheran family, my grandfather is the pastor at Trinity Lutheran Church in Durand, Illinois."

"Did you do any activities outside of school?"

"I played piano."

She kept reading Karen's file. "You have not chosen your majors yet."

"Yes, I know. That's why I'm here."

"Good, we can add them now. What are they?"

"My top choice is a dietetics degree; education is my second choice. I don't have a third choice."

"Okay, teaching makes sense, but dietetics? You don't have any background in this area," the counselor said, confused.

"My roommate is studying to become a doctor, and I'm currently taking the Introduction to Nutrition course. It's such an exciting field!"

"I see," the counselor said as she closed her file. "Karen, unfortunately, we do not offer a dietetics degree here at Concordia College. We offer a minor in Clinical Nutrition at our medical school, but you need to pursue a medical degree for this minor."

Chapter 3

"Oh," Karen replied.

"Have you taken any other courses? Don't stick to just one idea for your future. You should take other classes that interest you, like teaching or music," the counselor said, smiling. "As a freshman, you have lots of time to decide on your future career path. See what's out there!"

Karen wandered back to Livedalen Hall, the precise clip-clop of her heels reverberating through the empty hallways. The sound seemed to intensify the chill in her heart. *Why am I even here,* she thought, *if I can't get the degree I want.* She paused at the Social Hub, noticing a foreign exchange student whose face brightened upon seeing someone else. Karen smiled and waved as she took a seat by the window, watching the delicate snowflakes fall from the gray sky, which once again covered the campus with a soft white blanket.

She wondered what Georgene was doing today. She looked at the payphone banks and considered calling her. She was the lifeline she relied on during her darkest times—the one who truly understood her. But the idea quickly passed. Georgene had drifted away. John had turned the page, too. Karen had to forge her own path now.

"You should've called me, Karen," her roommate scolded.

"It's okay. The quiet gave me time to think," Karen responded. "I went to the library and learned more about nutrition and dietetics careers."

"So, what will you do if you can't get a degree here at Concordia?"

"Maybe I'll go back to the career counselor and ask about dietetics degrees at other schools. I can go anywhere. I was accepted at Columbia, and I would love to move to New York."

"I know they have an outstanding program at the University of Minnesota in St. Paul. It's ranked as one of the top dietetics programs in the United States."

"Interesting," Karen said.

"Why don't you call them and ask? The counselors want you to stay at Concordia College, so they will encourage you to consider their programs. That's not what you want."

"You're right! She tried to push me towards a teaching degree," Karen said, standing up. "I'm going to the library to find a phone number for the program at the University of Minnesota. Maybe I can talk to someone about their program."

"That's the spirit!"

Chapter 3

An hour later, she called the program counselor from a payphone in the Social Hub. Her roommate was right; their dietetics program was very comprehensive! After reviewing her notes from the library about what she needed to succeed as a dietitian, she realized this program offered everything she wanted. It had highly rated professors, a strong reputation, and a good clinical component. She also qualified for admission based on her high school grades and test scores. However, not all her credits from Concordia College would transfer to the University of Minnesota, and the counselor mentioned she would be a quarter behind her fellow freshmen. The silver lining was that she could attend summer school to complete the remaining prerequisite courses and catch up. The Nutrition and Dietetics Program was accepting applications for the fall semester. Still, she needed to act quickly, as the deadline for summer classes was the 31st of January.

"Are you going to apply?" her roommate asked after she returned to her dorm room.

Karen smiled and said, "They are mailing me the application materials today."

"Well, that's a shame they don't have a dietetics program at Concordia College," her grandpa said. "This is so sudden. I'd hate for you to leave such a good Lutheran school. Are you sure you want to move to St. Paul? You haven't even seen the school?"

"It is one of the best programs in the nation, Grandpa. I had to make a quick decision because the application deadline is at the end of January. I'm sure I will like the school," Karen replied, wrapping her finger around the metal payphone cord.

"What did your mother and father say about it?" he inquired.

"I haven't shared the news with them yet because I haven't been accepted, so there's not much to say about it."

"Well, you should tell them you're thinking about switching schools to pursue your dietetics degree," he said. "After all, they're still paying for your college, even though you had a big fight a couple of weeks ago."

Karen sighed. "You're right, Grandpa. I'll call them sometime and tell them."

"Praise the Lord."

A couple of months later, Karen strode back to Livedalen Hall, her face beaming after her final exam for Introduction to Nutrition. She knew, with absolute

Chapter 3

certainty, she'd nailed every answer. As she pushed through the double doors and logged her return, her gaze caught students hanging cardboard four-leaf clovers and signs proclaiming, "Happy St. Patrick's Day." Karen spotted a letter nestled in her mail slot—it was from the University of Minnesota. *This is it!* she thought. She ripped open the envelope and devoured the words: "Congratulations. You have been accepted into the University of Minnesota's Dietetics and Nutrition program at the St. Paul campus."

Karen looked up and smiled at her dormmates, laughing as they attempted to mimic an Irish accent. Her dream had just come true! She looked back at the letter.

"You will be assigned a dorm room in Bailey Hall, and summer classes will begin on June 2nd, 1962. If you pass your prerequisite summer courses, you will officially start the program during the Fall Quarter of 1962."

Chapter 4

There was a loud knock on Howard's dorm room door. "C'mon, Howard. Let's go! We're going to miss the bus!"

Howard rolled over and looked at his clock. It was 9:45 a.m.! He bolted out of bed and ripped off his pajamas.

The echoes of last night's date with Judy still reverberated in Howard's mind. On Wednesday, he had taken a chance, asking out a girl as beautiful as Judy after their Everyday Chemicals class. To his delight, she had eagerly agreed, suggesting they spend Friday night in her dorm.

Since the Friday night Bridge game was in full swing in the Bailey lobby, they'd decided to talk in her room. Judy and her roommate were quite popular, and throughout the night, friends kept popping their heads into their dorm room, interrupting Howard and Judy's date. Eventually, at midnight, they'd returned to the lobby to spend some time getting to know each other better. Judy's poised demeanor and engaging smile had left a lasting impression on Howard. Her family owned a successful restaurant in Des Moines, and she was studying interior design. The 2 a.m. curfew had forced them to end their conversation, despite his reluctance. They'd shared a sweet goodnight kiss before he headed back to Pioneer Hall.

Howard grabbed a black tie and made a half-Windsor knot, grabbed his overcoat and wallet, and ran down to the Pioneer lobby.

"About time!" Tom said. "We were about to leave without you."

"And miss the Iowa game?" Howard said. "No way. Not in a million years."

The commuter bus was packed with students going to the Brick. Howard and his friends had to stand.

"How was your date with Judy?" Tom asked as the bus stopped at Bailey Hall. Most students looked inside and decided to wait for the next bus.

Howard smiled. "Wonderful! She has such a vibrant personality. I'm enjoying getting to know her."

"She's from Des Moines, right?" Arthur asked.

"Yes, but don't hold that against her! She's not a football fan."

Of course, the Brick was sold out. Everyone in the United States wanted to go to this game. The only seats available were for students. They were cold wooden

Chapter 4

bleacher seats, but, hey, it was free if you showed your student ID card. Usually, if you got there before 11 a.m., you were guaranteed to get in, even during rivalry games. They arrived at 10:25 and joined the student lines.

A standing-room-only crowd of over 65,000 watched the Big Ten Championship game. The #3 ranked Golden Gophers stunned the #1 ranked Iowa Hawkeyes 27-10 on a brisk but sunny November afternoon. Howard and most other students rushed onto the field after the surprising victory as the Gophers received the Floyd of Rosedale trophy from their biggest rival.

"Wow! I still can't believe it!" Howard said, shaking his head and smiling. Everyone on the bus was still cheering and celebrating the victory.

Tom announced, "If we are selected for the Rose Bowl, I'm going. Who's with me?" A chorus of voices cried out, "Me!" "I'm in!" and "You betcha!" accompanied by raised arms and high-fives.

"I've never been to California," Howard said to Tom. "My parents went there for their honeymoon."

"Of course, you're going!" Tom said. "It wouldn't be the same without Boatman there!" as he high-fived more students on the bus.

Finding the One: A 1960s Love Story

Once his weekend obligation on the farm ended during planting season, Howard started working as a dishwasher at the Dining Center. Although the wages were meager, the free food pass was a welcome perk. He diligently saved, enabling him to acquire a used VW Beetle, which boasted superior fuel efficiency compared to the '52 Ford. The earnings offset gas costs, financed his textbooks, and even furnished some extra spending money for entertainment. Since many students on the St. Paul campus ate at the Dining Center, he became a familiar face around campus by the end of the quarter. As a result, he received invitations to the best parties and became a popular student.

"Sounds like you had a great freshman year!" Dick said as they sat in his brand new red 1961 Chevy Bel-Aire at the A&W in Lake City. "How did you like Los Angeles?"

"So much fun! The temperature was 60 degrees. We celebrated New Year's Eve at Disneyland, enjoying the fireworks at midnight. The following day, we watched the Rose Bowl Parade and attended the game. Unfortunately, the Gophers lost to Washington, but we still had a great time."

"Wow, how exciting!"

"How was your first year of seminary school at Concordia?" Howard asked.

"It was stressful. A ton of study and memorization. Hey, why didn't we ever meet up? You know, my campus is only a mile away from yours?"

"I know, I know. We should get together at least once a month," Howard replied.

"Agreed!"

A girl roller-skated to the driver's side of the Bel-Aire and hooked the tray to the window.

"Two cheeseburgers, fries, one vanilla, and one chocolate malt. The total..." she peeked inside the car at Howard and Dick. "Howard! How are you?"

Howard smiled at his old girlfriend. "I'm good, Mary. How are you?"

Mary played with her hair and smiled at Howard. "I'm great! I heard you and Dick were back in town for the summer. How is college life in the Twin Cities?"

"Fun, but busy. I went to Los Angeles for the Rose Bowl in January."

"Wow, what fun! I've never been to California. The only place you ever took me was to Red Wing at the St. James."

Chapter 4

Howard smiled at the memory. "Yes, I remember that night. We had a great time."

Two bells rang. "Well, back to work," she said with a smile before gliding away on her skates. Once she reached the sidewalk, she stopped, looked back at Howard, and glided to the passenger side of the car. Howard rolled down the window.

"Sorry, I almost forgot; the total is $3.25, guys," Mary said, feeling a bit embarrassed. Dick and Howard reached for their wallets and handed her $5.00.

"Keep the change, Mary," Howard said with a smile. Mary leaned down and kissed Howard on the cheek.

"Thanks, love," she smiled and glided away, giving Howard a playful grin.

"It looks like you are going to have a busy summer, Howard," Dick smiled as he handed Howard a cheeseburger and fries.

Howard laid out his mom's 100-foot garden hose next to the base of each tomato plant in her vegetable garden. He plugged in an electric hand drill with an orange extension cord and inserted a 1/8-inch drill bit. His parents watched him closely, clearly worried about what he was planning to do.

"Son, you tried to explain this over the phone one Sunday night. You want to use a drill to make holes in her garden hose and insert those little plastic things into it, right?" He held up a tiny rubber fitting. "How will the sprinkler water the garden if the hose is full of holes?"

Howard chuckled to himself as he explained. "We're putting together a drip irrigation system. A classmate and I were chatting about this one night over a beer. We'll hook up Mom's hose to the well and then attach a cap fitting to the other end. After that, we'll install some drip fittings along the hose right at each tomato plant's base."

"How often do they drip from the fitting?" Evelyn asked.

"Every few seconds."

His mother gasped. "That's not enough water, Howard! They will die. A plant requires water on its leaves and stem to grow, too. You can't just water the roots."

"Not necessarily. Watering with a sprinkler can promote the growth of fungus and disease on the plant. Remember what I told you about watering plants early in the morning? Have you been following that advice?"

"Well, when I think about it, yes," his mother replied. "But when the weather is dry, you need to

Chapter 4

water more often. As far back as I can remember, I've watered the garden three times a day during the scorching days of July—morning, afternoon, and evening. It's easy to remember: thirty minutes, three times a day."

Howard sighed. "With this method, you can water your plants three times a day, too, hitting the roots right where they need it. It saves water and keeps the weeds away."

Evelyn shook her head. "My tomato leaves will shrivel up and die without a sprinkler. Besides, we don't have to save water. We have a well."

Howard stood up. "Mom, listen. I'd like to try this. If I'm right, your tomatoes will produce bigger yields and larger crops than the ones fed by sprinklers."

"I really don't want you putting holes in my garden hose. What if this experiment flops? Please, do your experiments at school and leave my garden out of it."

"It *will* work, Mom."

Dad said, "The more important question is how this trivial experiment will help our production in the fields. Isn't it easier to use flood irrigation like we have for years?"

"First of all, flood irrigation promotes weeds. If the corn roots get all the water, the weeds don't get the moisture they need to grow."

Dad chuckled. "I can see why you like this idea. You always disliked hoeing the back 40."

Howard went on, "Second, better corn production. The constant water drip seeps deep into the soil, allowing the plant's roots to dig deeper, which means a healthier and more productive stalk. Plus, less water use."

"Son, we have more than enough water. This well is deep and has been reliable for years."

"You're right. However, long-term projections indicate that there will be less water available in southwestern Minnesota. Everyone needs to conserve as much water as possible to support the underground water levels. This is a wise decision for the future of this farm, and that's exactly why you're funding my education. So, can I show you how it works?" he asked, holding up the drill.

On his mom's kitchen counter, a large pile of fresh, ripe tomatoes sat next to quart-sized Mason jars and a box of fresh seals. Two large stock pots of water boiled on the gas stove, the bubbling heat transforming the kitchen into an oppressive sauna. One pot blanched the tomatoes, which Howard kept a close eye on, while the other pot held Mason jars filled with skinless tomatoes.

Chapter 4

Across the kitchen, his mom peeled the hot tomato skins and placed the pulp into jars with a large-rimmed funnel. She sealed two jars and joined Howard next to the stove.

"We're almost halfway through," she said, taking a towel and removing two jars from the boiling water, setting them on the kitchen table. "I'm glad you're helping me today. The tomatoes have gone crazy this year, and it's much easier with another pair of hands."

"It's good to be here, Mom," he replied, looking over at his mother. "My tomato-watering experiment seems to be working!"

"Yes, it did. How are things between you and the Wainwright girl? What's her name..."

"Mary, her name is Mary, Mom."

"Yes, that's it. You two went out again last night. What did you do?" she asked, putting two new jars into the boiling water.

Howard used a ladle to scoop out two more blanched tomatoes and placed them on a cutting board. "We had dinner at the Terrace and watched some bands," he said.

"Did you have a good time? You were out until very early this morning," she replied, taking the cutting board to her station. "And you were dozing off during the sermon today."

"Yes, Paster Otto gave me a disapproving look after the service."

"You two have gone out almost every weekend since you came home. Are things getting serious between you two?" she smiled at him as she returned the cutting board.

"Mom, we were serious in high school, but we're just close friends now. We've had frank discussions about it. If I weren't so far away, our relationship would inevitably grow closer. But we know August is coming."

His mom peeled the skin off the blanched tomatoes. "I know, dear. I was just wondering if there's something serious between the two of you. Do you have any girlfriends in the Cities?"

"There is one girl, Judy. I like her. But I am very busy with my studies and working at the Dining Center. There is not much time for dating."

"Of course. School comes first," she replied as she returned with two more jars of tomatoes.

"What did you do over the summer, Judy?" Howard yelled, handing her a plastic cup filled with wapatoolie. The party was in full swing. As a new pledge of Alpha Gamma Rho, he was responsible for the big steel bin

Chapter 4

full of the colorful drink. For the last three hours, he'd been working hard to make sure the mix of fresh fruit and alcohol was just right, passing out cups and ladling the punch into excited hands. He made sure everyone was having a good time, especially his potential fraternity brothers. They were to make their decision the following week.

Judy looked classy in a tan tie-belt dress and white pillbox hat. Her eyes sparkled as she spoke to Howard. "I returned to my parents' house in Des Moines and worked at their restaurant over the summer. How about you?"

"The same. I mean, I helped my dad on the farm," he replied.

"Hey, there you are!" A guy walked up and wrapped his hands around her waist. They exchanged a quick kiss, leaving Howard bewildered.

"Oh, how rude. Howard, this is Michael," she shouted. "I met him over the summer in Des Moines."

Michael extended his hand toward Howard. "You're Howard Boatman, right? Judy mentioned you," he hollered, giving Howard a forceful handshake. "You're pursuing an ag degree. You're a farmer, right?"

"Yeah," Howard replied, looking confused as he glanced at Judy. Michael held out his glass, and Howard added a ladle of wapatoolie.

"Is it true that farmers have sex with their animals?" he shouted. "I mean, not you specifically, but like, farmers in general?"

"Stop, Michael!" Judy declared, shaking her head as she wrapped her arms around his waist. "Michael and I met at my parents' restaurant when he came in one day with his friends," she said, smiling at him. "He has been accepted to the Law School at Fraser Hall."

Michael smiled at Judy. "I like to joke that I came in for pie and left with something much sweeter." Judy giggled and slapped Michael on the arm.

"Wow. That's great, Judy," Howard said flatly.

"Jude, I want you to meet one of my law school buddies," Michael said, grabbing her waist and pulling her away. She glanced back at Howard and shot him a smile as Michael pinched her on the butt. Howard froze, the ladle dripping wapatoolie onto the floor as he watched them disappear into the fraternity.

"Hey, wapatoolie boy!" one of the brothers said, holding out his glass. "A little help here?"

After the harvest season on the farm in October, Howard was rehired as the dishwasher in the Dining Center. This job fit well with his class schedule, which

Chapter 4

primarily consisted of morning classes. He also joined the Ag Club, the largest club on the Saint Paul campus.

A youthful energy swept across the United States, fueled by President Kennedy's New Frontier, which was known for its innovation and global leadership. This progressive vision made Howard eager for his second year at St. Paul. Like most 200-level courses at the University of Minnesota, his classes emphasized imagination and out-of-the-box thinking. The School of Agriculture was a prominent example of the changing times. Led by revolutionary ideas developed by faculty and students, many of these concepts were implemented by farmers across the United States and around the world.

One fundamental course was Food Science and Agricultural Chemistry, taught by Dr. George, a highly respected expert in the field of agriculture. His publication, "Ag-Science for the 20th Century," was widely regarded as the farmer's Bible. Additionally, Dr. George's column in Ag Monthly was read by millions in the agricultural industry. The classes were only available to sophomore-level students or higher at the School of Agriculture and always filled up quickly.

Clinton Black taught a course titled "What If – Economic Alchemy in the New Frontier." He had served as Secretary of Agriculture under President Truman in the 1940s and had played a pivotal role in revolutionizing farming techniques following World War II. His innovative thinking significantly contributed to feeding the people of Europe during the Marshall Plan. In his course description, Professor Black wrote the following:

This class focuses on creativity and financial problem-solving in the agricultural community. If you wish to learn the basics about economics and farm management, this course is not for you.

At 9 a.m. on the first day of class, Professor Black wrote on the board, "Imagination is more important than knowledge."

"If you take away just one lesson from this course, let it be this quote from my late friend Albert Einstein. Please reflect on its meaning," he said. "Tomorrow, you will share your thoughts with the class. Dismissed."

Professor Black collected his belongings, oblivious of the students' deflated expressions as they shared telling glances. No one budged. Professor Black paused, his gaze sweeping across the room.

"Okay, tell me: what is one thing you learned about running a farming business?" He stood there, waiting for a response. "Anyone?"

One student replied, "Farming depends on the weather."

"Absolutely. So, how can you control the weather?" he asked.

Chapter 4

Howard scoffed and said, "You can't control the weather."

Professor Black pointed at Howard and said, "I want you to think of a way to control the weather by tomorrow at 9 a.m."

He continued, "In 1946, President Truman presented me with a daunting challenge: 'We need to feed over 400 million Europeans while still providing for 140 million Americans here at home. I want three proposals on my desk in a week.' It felt nearly impossible, but we allowed imagination to take the lead over mere knowledge. With the ideas from my team, we successfully fed Europe for three years."

"Next on our agenda is a call for proposals," announced the president of the Ag Club. "The family farm in the United States is facing its biggest threat ever; it is no longer a profitable industry. Many family farmers have been forced to sell their farms, some of which have been passed down through generations, to large corporations. As a result, there has been a significant decline in the number of family-owned farms over the last 20 years. Some of you may have witnessed this firsthand with friends and neighbors while growing up.

"While the New Frontier has driven innovation across many industries worldwide, the agriculture sector—especially family farms—has faced significant challenges. As students learning from some of the leading experts in agriculture, we are in a prime position to affect change. Our professors encourage us to think creatively, and as future leaders of the industry, it is essential that we do just that.

"I encourage each of you to submit proposals that support family farm ownership. The deadline for submissions is November 1. We will present these proposals to the faculty and ask for their feedback. Discussion."

"Is it possible to submit more than one proposal?" one club member inquired.

"Absolutely," the president replied.

"This is the kind of problem-solving that makes our country great," another member commented.

Howard sat next to him, reflecting on the drip irrigation experiment he'd conducted with his mom's garden last summer.

"I move to form an initiative aimed at creating strategic proposals to support and promote the future of family farm ownership," stated a member of the club.

"Second," three people called out.

Chapter 4

"Okay, there is a motion and a second," the president said. "All those in favor?"

An enthusiastic chorus of 'ayes' filled the room.

"Class dismissed. Don't forget about the field trip on Monday," Dr. George announced to the class, directing his gaze toward Howard. "Howard, please stop by my office after lunch today."

"Sure, Doctor," Howard replied, intrigued.

At 1 p.m., Howard found Dr. George sitting with Professor Black in his office. He rapped softly on the door. "You asked to see me?"

"Yes, Howard, please join us," he replied as Professor Black turned to look at him. "We have been discussing the proposals that the Ag Club submitted earlier this week. Please, have a seat." Dr. George then pulled out Howard's proposal on distributing organic fertilizer using drip irrigation.

"All of these ideas have been the highlight of the faculty's week. Everyone was surprised by the initiative and the number of proposals aimed at promoting family farm ownership," he paused and picked up Howard's proposal.

Chapter 4

"But your ideas on organic fertilization using drip irrigation were exceptional, Howard. While many ideas were unique, they often lacked concrete implementation solutions. You developed a distinctive concept and outlined practical plans along with the necessary equipment for a 100-acre farm. Professor Black studied the initial financial investment and the 10-year prospects of your proposal."

"The initial investment is significant, Howard," started Professor Black, "but this plan could save a family farm thousands of dollars starting in the fourth year. It can also be applied to larger corporate farms with a shorter breakeven period. When combined with a well-structured loan program, this could lead to financial success for farms of any size. Well done!"

Dr. George continued, "Yesterday, we forwarded your proposal to Dean Gordon. This morning before class, he visited my office to request a pitch for the 1962 growing season."

"A pitch for... what?" Howard asked, eyes wide.

"An internship in the experimental fields. The dean told me that Professor Waterford has a quarter-acre of land available for 1962. Professor Black and I were tossing around some ideas for your experiment. We propose to split the field in half. One side will be our control area with flood irrigation and spray equipment for liquid fertilizer. The other half will be the experimental area, where you and your team will set up the drip irrigation tubing system for irrigation and fertilizer. You will need to keep detailed records of water and fertilizer use for each section. What do you think of our idea to split these into two lots?"

"Yeah," Howard said, hardly believing his ears. "Of course."

"Good. Dean Gordon wants you to share your pitch with the department heads on Monday at 3:00 p.m. in the conference room. For this presentation, you are required to include a feasibility summary, as well as short and long-term impacts on the agricultural industry, and an annual budget for the project that covers salaries for four employees. You need to prepare 12 handouts for each faculty member. Can you do it?"

"The... whole department?" Howard asked.

"You have to defend your pitch to the department after your presentation. Experimental field internships require a unanimous vote from the faculty."

"Yes, um... of course," Howard stuttered.

"And you believe the experiment will work in a real situation?" his dad asked over the phone on Sunday.

Chapter 4

"It worked well in Mom's garden during the summer," Howard replied. "I believe it could also work on a larger scale."

"When is your presentation?" he asked.

"Tomorrow at 3 p.m., the entire faculty will be there."

His mom added. "Your confidence in the proposal shines through your body language. Don't forget that. And remember, no spelling errors!"

"I'm looking forward to reading all about it in Ag Monthly," his dad replied.

The faculty selected three pitches for oral presentations. The first pitch was for a government grant program aimed at promoting sustainable agricultural practices and enhancing water conservation efforts within the farming community. The second proposed no-interest farm loans for land and equipment to family farms with an acreage of under 100 acres. The final presentation featured Howard's ideas on organic crop fertilization using drip irrigation.

The faculty unanimously approved all three pitches. Each financial proposal would be presented by the respective student to the Minnesota Department of Agriculture for consideration, highlighting the school's commitment to innovation and sustainability. Additionally, Howard's proposal was selected for the

Experimental Fields during the 1962 growing season. He was also approved for an internship starting in the winter quarter and was granted three employees to assist with the project. Dr. George and Mr. Waterford would be serving as advisors.

"Castro is definitely a communist," his dad said. "But I'm concerned about how close Cuba is to the U.S. mainland. If he succeeds in taking over Cuba, having a communist country 90 miles away from the United States could cause trouble."

"I agree with you," Dick's father replied. "But it's such a backward country that I don't think they will pose a real threat to us. What are they going to do, launch a military attack with their army of 200 troops and invade Florida?" Everyone laughed.

The ladies called from the kitchen. "Dinner's ready, guys."

"So, do you boys have plans tonight?" Dick's father asked as Howard took a bite of meatloaf.

"We are going on a double date to the Terrace," Dick said. "There are some great live bands tonight and for New Year's Eve on Monday."

Chapter 4

"How is school going, Howard? Your father tells me you were granted a research project at the University."

"Yes, starting in spring quarter, I'm leading an experiment on the effectiveness of organic fertilization in drip irrigation systems," he replied. "Similar to the irrigation experiment in Mom's garden last season."

"Impressive," he said.

"Yes, but time-consuming. I must stay on campus to oversee the project."

"Oh, how will that affect your farming duties here?" he asked.

Howard lowered his head and took another bite of his meatloaf.

"He won't be coming back next season," Howard's dad declared, his voice heavy with finality.

An oppressive silence descended upon the table, stretching for what felt like an eternity. Howard ached for a shift in topic, the echo of his father's harsh admonishment still ringing in his ears from earlier that day.

His mother grabbed the empty basket of butter rolls and stood up. "Well, these were popular."

His dad looked at Howard and said, "He has shown me how this works and how I could implement it here at home. He is excited about this experiment. If it's successful, it could have a significant impact on water conservation nationwide. I'm considering the project as well, especially if I can secure a grant through the Department of Agriculture. Since this is so important, I told him he could skip helping on the farm this season." He looked at Howard and added, "He will come home to help whenever he can. In the meantime, I will hire the Anderson boy to assist me full-time this year."

"After dinner, can you show me how this works, Howard?" Dick's dad asked.

Dick snagged a parking spot along Highway 61 as Howard pulled the lawn chairs out of the back seat. Just like always, Lake City was packed with people from the Twin Cities, making it feel like a complete madhouse. Howard felt like one of them, even though he had lived in Lake City all his life. Even so, he was happy to escape the experiment for the holiday weekend.

"Looks like our spot is still open," Dick remarked as they approached the grassy knoll near the bluffs. "It's almost 9 p.m.; I guess we got lucky." They settled into their lawn chairs, embracing the moment as they watched the array of boats in the serene waters of Lake Pepin. The waterfront buzzed with laughter and cheerful chatter as families and friends gathered to enjoy the lively evening. Colorful picnic blankets were

Chapter 4

spread out on the freshly cut grass. In the distance, a lively brass band played *America the Beautiful*, filling the air with a sense of nostalgia and national pride. Children raced around, laughing and shouting as they waved small American flags, adding to the festive atmosphere.

They had been watching the fireworks show in Lake City since they were little, and now that they were in college in the Twin Cities, it brought back many memories. While everything felt familiar and comfortable, there was also a noticeable sense of detachment, reminding them of how much they had outgrown Lake City.

"Howard, I have some big news to share with you," Dick said as he stared at the boats. "I wasn't sure when to bring this up, but now seems like a good time."

"What's up, Dick? Everything okay?" Howard looked at his friend, concerned, as two kids darted between their lawn chairs.

Dick sighed. "My family is going to lose the farm."

"What! Why? What happened?"

"As you know, the low crop prices last season affected everyone in Goodhue County," he started.

"Yeah, my dad felt it, too."

"In the spring, the International finally broke down completely. My dad applied for a loan with Lake City

Bank to buy a new tractor, but it was denied due to excessive debt-to-income ratios. My brothers and I pooled our resources to buy a used tractor from the implement shop in Red Wing. It was all the money we had. Now, even though my brothers started working at the grain elevator here in town, our family can no longer make the monthly loan payments. I returned from Concordia in June and attempted to negotiate a buyout, but my request was denied due to my student loans. I even considered quitting seminary school," he said, looking down at his hands. "The bank told us last week that there will be an auction."

"No! You have lived there all your life, Dick! They can't take it away. What if you and your brothers apply for a loan together? With their jobs, surely the bank will give you guys a loan?"

"Lake City Bank considered that, too. There is just too much debt, Howard."

"What is your family going to do?" Howard asked, his wide eyes staring in disbelief.

"With the auction proceeds, my mom and dad are going to buy a house in Lake City and retire."

"And you and your brothers lose the farm," Howard said.

"Yeah."

Chapter 4

After a few seconds, a resounding boom echoed through the calm evening sky. As the cheers and applause filled the air, the two lifelong friends wore a funeral-like expression, as though Marshal Dillon had just passed away. Howard looked over at his oldest friend, his heart aching as he saw a tear glistening on his cheek, illuminated by the warm glow of the fireworks.

"Hey, let's go over to the A&W, Dick! What do you say?" Howard asked after the fireworks finale. "My treat."

He glanced at Dick and understood the look in his eyes. Every farm boy dreams of one day owning the family farm, but Dick knew that his family's dream was now over. He was still struggling to come to terms with this new reality.

Yet, even in this moment of despair, Dick turned to him and replied with a hopeful voice, "Sure, Howard."

The drive-in was crowded, but they found an open spot after a few minutes. They ordered their usual: two cheeseburgers, fries, one vanilla malt, and one chocolate malt.

Howard wondered if Mary still worked as a waitress. *Nah, I doubt it*, he thought. *At 20 years old, she's probably too old to be a waitress at a drive-in.*

However, as they discussed the Vikings' chances for the upcoming season, Mary glided around the corner on her skates.

"Two cheeseburgers, fries, one vanilla, and one chocolate malt. That will be…"

"$3.25," Howard said, smiling at Mary.

Mary jumped, hearing Howard's voice. "Howard! You're home?"

Howard smiled. "Yes, only for the holiday, though. How are you, Mary?"

"I'm great… just great, Howard," she said, looking at the ground. "I'm so surprised to see you."

"And I'm surprised you're still working here."

"Yeah, one of the girls called in sick, so we had to cover her shift," she said.

"We?" Howard asked.

"Oh… yeah, we," she glanced around and let out a sigh. "I guess I should be the one to tell you, right? Brian and I run the A&W now."

"You bought this place? Wow, congratulations!"

"No, Howard. Brian is my fiancé."

"What?!" he blurted, his jaw clenched as his smile vanished. Finally, he managed, "Isn't he too old for you?"

Chapter 4

"Yeah, he's 42 years old," she snapped and quickly added, "but he owns Stout Cottage and the A&W. We've been dating for a few months."

She's engaged to someone who is 22 years older than her? he thought. *This doesn't make any sense.*

"Okay, it's $3.25," she said, calling out to another waitress as she rolled by. "Carol, can you please take the order for bay 22? I'm a little busy right now."

"Sure, Mary," she replied, staring at Howard.

He reached into his pocket and handed her $5.00. "When were you going to tell me, Mary?"

Mary sighed as she leaned into the driver's side window, locking eyes with Howard. "I know this isn't easy for you, and I'm sorry. Just know that we are happy together," she said, rubbing her temple. "I'm 20 now, and it's a small town. You haven't called or written, and you haven't been home in months. Honestly, Howard, I've just grown tired of waiting for you to commit."

She gave him a lackluster smile, straightened up, and casually glided away from Howard's life.

On Sunday night, Howard was stuck in a long line of cars at a red light in Red Wing. It had been a rough weekend, and he couldn't shake the thought that neither Mary nor Dick would be around after graduation.

Driving north on Highway 61, just beyond Cottage Grove, he was stopped by a herd of cows crossing the road. A flash of inspiration hit him as the cattle meandered past. He put the car in park and retrieved his briefcase. His mind was running faster than his pen. He was so absorbed that he didn't realize the herd had already moved on and drivers were honking at his VW Beetle.

He couldn't believe he hadn't thought of this sooner! He needed to run the financials and develop a marketing plan, but he realized that targeting small grocery stores and individual customers in Rochester would be more profitable than selling directly to slaughterhouses. The cattle industry was thriving, and with his prime location in Goodhue County and his expertise, he believed he could recover his investment in under a year.

After numerous drafts, he viewed his proposal as a way to secure a stable financial future for his family's farm. In the long run, corn and soybeans would help repay the loans, while meat processing would become the primary source of income. However, the challenge was in sales. For the initial years, Howard would also have to take on the role of a salesperson. Sales professionals spend countless hours building relationships, and with the need to manage both cornfields and livestock, he would have to hire someone to take over his farm duties.

He valued the peace that came with driving a tractor, tending to animals, and enjoying the invigorating fresh air. He longed for that lifestyle again while attending the University of Minnesota. Sales and marketing were not his forte; farming was his true passion. He couldn't imagine a career without it.

Chapter 5

"Look, I can't. To catch up with my classmates in the dietetics program, I have to attend summer classes," Karen said into the payphone while her roommate listened nearby.

"I don't know, Dad," Karen continued, "next week I finish my finals here in Moorhead. Then, I have a week before classes start in St. Paul. That's not much time for me to get settled into Bailey Hall. And it's a long bus ride to Rockford—eight hours."

She ended the call a few minutes later and hung up the payphone.

"So," her roommate said. "What did they say?"

"My grandpa told them that I was accepted into the program, but they were disappointed I couldn't come home over the summer. They invited me to go shopping at the new Oakbrook Center Mall in Chicago over the Fourth of July. They got a hotel room."

"Well, that sounds like a good idea, Karen," her roommate said as they started walking back to Livedalen Hall.

Karen glared at her. "No, I won't endure a grueling bus ride to Rockford just to… do what? Spend time with people I don't want to see?"

"Remember, they are paying for your school," her roommate reminded her.

Karen smiled. "You sound like my grandfather."

The sight of her roommate's enthusiastic wave from the sidewalk brought a loving smile to Karen's face. As the bus pulled away for St. Paul, Karen settled into her seat. *I'm on my way,* she thought. *A new school. A new city. A new start.*

As she gazed out the window at the endless rows of cornfields, she found herself lost in thought, reflecting on her life. Georgene had been her closest friend through high school. But now, distance and time had changed their friendship. John was now with someone else. Even though they were still friends, it felt different with this new girl in the picture. And although she and her roommate were close, Karen felt their bond fading amid the chaos of the bus station.

Looking around the bus, a crushing realization hit her: apart from her family, she had no one to turn to. A desolate loneliness sank into her heart.

Chapter 5

How did I end up so alone? she thought, the question resounding in her mind like a haunting whisper. Her gaze drifted to the endless fields of cornstalks whipping past, then sharpened, plant by plant, on the individual stalks. Each one stood proud yet lonely amidst the teeming masses, a poignant reflection of her own isolation in a bustling world.

Yet, as they approached the vibrant pulse of the Twin Cities, a flicker of hope ignited within her. *This is the beginning of a new chapter in my life*, she mused, her eyes drinking in the kaleidoscope of possibilities that awaited her as the skyline of Minneapolis and St. Paul drew closer.

Suitcase in hand, Karen waited in the endless queue, her vulnerability magnified by the intimidating presence of predominantly male students.

"Karen Smith," she said to the resident assistant as she reached the front of the line. She placed her suitcase down while he searched for her name on a sheet of paper.

"Ahh, yes. You're the woman from Concordia College, right?" he asked, looking up at her.

"Yes, I just arrived a few minutes ago."

"You have been assigned Room 317 in Bailey Hall," he said, standing up. He grabbed keys from the "317 Bailey" cubbyhole and sat back down. "Bailey Hall is an all-women's dormitory. Here's your room key. You get one room key, and replacements cost five dollars, so don't lose it," he warned.

He placed a handbook on the table. "This is the University of Minnesota General Handbook. On pages five and six, you will find the rules for women," he paused and looked her straight in the eye. "If you do not comply with the rules, you will be brought before RA Court, where we will determine your punishment, up to and including expulsion from the university," he said as Karen picked up the handbook.

At Concordia, every woman was required to check in before midnight. Skirts could not be above the knee. No men were allowed in the women's dorm rooms, not even family. And everyone in Livedalen Hall was subject to random cleanliness checks. She felt relieved that she no longer had to follow these rules. But now, a new uncertainty gnawed at her —was this place any different?

The RA handed Karen a sheet of paper labeled "General Rules Acknowledgment."

"Please sign here," he said, pointing to the bottom of the legal form and handing Karen a pen. Karen signed

Chapter 5

the form; the RA looked carefully at her signature and filed it away.

"You're currently in the St. Paul Student Center, the SPSC. Next door is the Dining Center. In winter, you can use the skyway to avoid going outdoors." He handed Karen a food card. "This is your temporary food card. On Sunday, you'll get a new card with your name. Bailey Hall is about a block north and west of the SPSC." He handed her a map. "This will help you find your way around campus. When you find Bailey Hall, introduce yourself to the head resident for more details. Any questions?"

A few minutes later, as she admired the sheer size of her new school, she found Bailey Hall. It was clear who the head resident was—an older student with a clipboard, surrounded by excited freshmen. She met every question with a calm, confident answer, as Karen and the others absorbed her every word. Karen set down her suitcase, waited her turn, and finally introduced herself.

"Karen Smith, 317," she said.

"Hi, Karen. I'm Julie," the woman said while she looked up her name. "Your roommate is already here;

she checked in yesterday. Her name is Patty. Did you get the handbook when you checked in at SPSC?"

Karen pulled out the handbook from her bag. "Yes, I did. I also had to sign some acknowledgment, too."

"Perfect. Any questions?"

"Yes. How strict are the rules here? The guy who checked me in mentioned this place called RA Court."

Julie shook her head and smiled. "That's Robert. He's one of the RAs. He's a stickler for the rules and lets his position go to his head. Don't worry about him. We dated for about a month when we were sophomores. I have been the head resident of Bailey Hall since it opened in 1959. He knows I look after my Bailey girls, and they don't wind up before Robert."

Karen gave Julie a smile. "At Concordia College, the rules were strict. No boys in your room, we couldn't wear skirts above the knee, and we had Cleanliness Checks."

Julie laughed. "Wait, you aren't allowed to have men in your room at all?"

"No men were allowed. They could only go into the lobby. Not even my dad was permitted to go up to my room."

"What are Cleanliness Checks?"

"They were allowed to search our room at any time to ensure it was clean. We were not permitted to have

Chapter 5

messy rooms. Usually, they conducted a Cleanliness Check on Saturday nights at curfew."

"Hilarious," Julie laughed. "I've heard that Concordia was tough. Karen, the rules are simple here. Of course, no alcohol or drugs in the dorms. The curfew is at midnight on weekdays and 2:00 a.m. on Friday and Saturday nights. At curfew, no men are allowed in your room," Julie pointed to the handbook in Karen's hand. "The guidelines include the dress code, and you can wear skirts above the knee on campus. You'll find Bailey Hall much more relaxed compared to Concordia."

Karen ascended to the third floor, eager to see her room and meet her new roommate. As she located room 317, the door across the hall swung open, and a striking sophomore with shoulder-length hair stepped into the hallway.

"Hi," she said. "Are you looking for Patty?" She looked down and noticed Karen's suitcase. "Oh, are you her new roommate?"

Karen smiled. "Yes. I'm Karen."

"Cool! My name's Ellie. It's nice to meet you," she yelled into the room. "Jan, get out here. Patty's roommate finally arrived."

"Where are you from?" Ellie asked as Karen set down her suitcase.

"I transferred from Concordia College in Morehead. It's in northern Minnesota near the North Dakota border."

"No way. You went to Concordia?" Ellie asked as Jan appeared in the doorway. Jan, a bit older than Ellie, had a more studious vibe, but both girls radiated a natural beauty.

"I started as a freshman at Concordia," Karen responded.

"We both grew up in Morehead!" Jan answered. "I'm Jan."

"Hi Jan, nice to meet you, I'm Karen." She could see the relationship between the two sisters. Jan was a little taller, but Ellie had nice skin and great hair.

"So, are you from Morehead?" Jan asked. "I've never seen you before."

"No, I'm originally from Rockford, Illinois. I started at Concordia last fall."

Ellie smiled. "Did you ever get to the Dairy Queen in town? Morehead's big claim to fame is the Dilly Bar. It was invented there."

Chapter 5

"Really?" Karen said. "I didn't have a car and never had any dates at that drive-in, but I've heard of it."

"Is it true that you couldn't wear skirts above the knee on campus?" Ellie asked.

"Yes, it's true. And women weren't permitted to enter men's dorm rooms, and men were not allowed to visit ours."

"I've heard that before," Jan said. "The opposite sex was only allowed to stay in the lobby of a dorm. That rule has existed since women first got admitted to Concordia."

"We used to go play mini golf, too. Do you remember?" Jan asked Ellie and looked at Karen. "It sounds weird, but it was the cool thing to do during the summer in high school then."

Karen's dorm room door opened to reveal a sophomore sporting an Audrey Hepburn look. "What's going on, Ellie?"

"Patty, this is Karen, your new roommate! I was just heading to the library when she showed up."

"Hello! Nice to meet you! I'm Patty," she said, glancing at her suitcase. "Would you like to see your room?"

"I thought you'd never ask!" Karen responded as the four of them entered her new home. She looked around while the other girls sat down on the beds.

"It's bigger than my room at Concordia," Karen remarked, sitting next to Ellie on the bed.

"You're OK with that side of the room?" Patty asked.

"Sure, it doesn't matter to me," Karen said.

"So, what's your story, Karen…"

Karen started to unpack and choose an outfit for the meet-and-greet at the Student Center after supper. Most of her clothes were wrinkled, so Ellie let her borrow her Pierre Cardin. They wore the same size. They finished getting ready and headed to the Dining Center.

"Wow, what a fantastic selection of food!" Karen exclaimed as she sat down with her new friends. There were about a dozen Bailey girls at the table.

Ellie spoke up. "Everyone, this is Karen. She lives with Patty in 317." Everyone waved and said, "Hi, Karen!"

"Where are you from, Karen?" one of them asked.

"Rockford, Illinois. It's an hour outside of Chicago."

"How do you like Minnesota so far?" another one asked.

Chapter 5

"The weather is great during the summer, but winters here are very cold with too much snow." Everyone chuckled.

Karen looked around the dining center and noticed that there were probably close to 100 people enjoying supper, yet her table was the only one with women. "Why are there so many men on campus?" Karen asked. "I noticed it when I checked in as well; I was the only girl in line."

"My dear, you are on the Ag side of the University of Minnesota," one of them commented. "Most of the guys are farmers or in the agricultural field. On the Minneapolis side, it is about 50/50."

"Advantage—us!" Patty said. Everyone laughed.

"Karen, that dress is cute. Is that Pierre Cardin?"

"Yes, it's Ellie's dress," Karen smiled at her friend. "All my clothes were wrinkled from the trip today."

"I found it at Frank Murphy," Ellie added.

"What's Frank Murphy?" Karen asked.

"It's one of our favorite clothing stores here in Saint Paul. Let's go over there tomorrow after we sign up for classes and go shopping!"

"I want to go, too," Patty added. "I need another dress."

As the only female dorm on the St. Paul campus, Bailey girls received a lot of attention. When the group walked into the North Star Ballroom, nearly every head turned.

"Wow, check out all the guys!" one of them whispered. Most were dressed in suits, challenging Karen's stereotype of college-aged farmers in overalls, boots, and straw hats. As they waited for the event to start, their group was the center of attention in the room. A few guys came up and said hello.

A few minutes later, Robert got on the microphone. "Welcome, everyone! And a special welcome to all of our freshmen and transfers. I'm Robert, one of the resident assistants on the Saint Paul campus. I'm excited to be here tonight to introduce our amazing staff and play some icebreaker games! Let's get started!"

Robert handed the microphone to the other two resident assistants and the five other head residents on campus, including Julie at Bailey Hall. The girls cheered when Julie introduced herself.

"Now we're going to play Human Bingo," Robert announced. "We've all played bingo before, but in this game, we won't be calling out numbers. Instead, each square on your bingo card contains a trait, experience, or hobby. Your task is to find someone who matches the description in each square. When you find a match, that person will write their name on your card. The first

person to complete a line—whether horizontal, vertical, or diagonal—will shout 'Bingo!'" The head residents began to pass out the bingo sheets. "Good luck, everyone!"

Ellie chuckled. "I wonder if 'milked a cow' is included. We shouldn't have trouble finding a guy who has done that in this room."

Another girl chimed in, "or 'drives a tractor to school!'" The others burst into muffled laughter.

After playing Human Bingo, the group played Birthday Boggle. The challenge was simple: everyone had five minutes to arrange themselves in a birthday sequence, without uttering a single word.

There was a pause as the staff prepared for the next icebreaker. Patty came up to Karen.

"Ellie just got invited to a house party. Are you in?"

"When?"

"Right now. Let's go!"

"Are we allowed to leave?" Karen asked.

Patty shook her head and laughed as she grabbed Karen's arm. Jan and Ellie were waiting outside the SPSC.

"He said just to follow the music," Ellie said.

They strolled past mansions adorned with large Greek letters on the side, all locked up and quiet for the

Chapter 5

summer. But just beyond the mansions, a smaller house was alive with vibrant sounds and energy.

As they went inside, all eyes turned toward them, captivated by Ellie's radiant and bubbly personality. With natural charm, she began to flirt, her confidence sparkled like a diamond and infused the room with an infectious spirit. Karen and the other girls joined in, embracing the jubilant vibe that surrounded them. Like SPSC, the party was attended mainly by guys, but this gathering had something special—a keg!

It wasn't long before Karen found herself talking with lots of guys. Most of them hailed from farms in Minnesota, Wisconsin, and Iowa.

"So, you're a crop duster?" she asked one of the guys as she took a drag from her cigarette. "I've heard that's dangerous work." He was very handsome in a suit coat and black wavy hair. He had a sexy voice, too.

"It can be hazardous if you're not hyper-vigilant," he smiled. "The danger lies in flying at high speed near the ground. You must be careful of all sorts of obstacles, such as power lines."

Another man joined the conversation. "I had a friend who was killed when his tractor rolled over on him. He was 17 years old."

"Oh, how awful!" Karen said.

A little while later, Jan found her. "Karen, we gotta go. It's a little before midnight."

"Already?" Karen replied.

"Yes, already," she said, eyeing the group of men talking to her. "Say 'good night' and let's go."

"Sorry, boys. Bye!" Karen said as Jan pulled her away.

Karen glanced at the moon hanging fat and low in the sky. "How can it be almost midnight already?" The others exchanged worried looks but did not explain as their heels scrambled back towards Bailey.

After waiting in line, they checked in five minutes before midnight and climbed up to the third floor. The stairs were buzzing with men and women coming and going. They kicked off their heels and left the dorm room door open.

"That was fun!" Karen said. "We didn't have parties like that at Concordia."

Patty looked at Ellie. "Just wait till she goes to a frat party. We will have to drag her out."

"Ohh, look at this one, Karen!" Ellie said as she held up a Foale and Tuffin mini dress with big bold lines.

Chapter 5

Karen examined the dress. "That would look great on you, Ellie. The colors match your skin tone and hair, and the print really flatters your body. You should try that one on."

Ellie smiled. "I think I will. Yeah. Thanks, Karen. I have a couple of Foale and Tuffin dresses back at Bailey. I love their slogan, 'We don't wanna be chic; we just wanna be ridiculous.'"

"I've heard they're quite unconventional. That matches your style."

Patty walked over to the girls. "How about this one?" she asked, holding an olive-green Christian Dior against her body.

Karen looked up and down the Dior. "I like the dress cut for you, but I don't like the color," Karen said. "That color makes your face look pale."

"I agree," the sales consultant said. "That color doesn't look right. Perhaps I can help you find another color in Dior?"

As they walked away, Ellie said, "Karen, you're really great at this!" She turned and looked Karen directly in the eye. "From now on, you're going to be my fashion consultant."

"Deal!"

Karen discovered a beautiful Mary Quant mod dress and a Givenchy mini dress perfect for parties. While she loved both dresses, she couldn't afford to buy them. However, with her new social calendar, Karen realized she needed to enhance her wardrobe. She decided to take a mental picture of the Mary Quant dress so she could sew a similar one back at Bailey.

"Who is your professor for Life Cycle Nutrition?" Jan asked.

"Let me see," Karen said as she looked through her notes. "Dawson."

"Uff da. That's the instructor I had. Dr. Dawson is tough," Jan said as she stood up, selecting a book from her bookshelf. "This is the textbook he used in my class last year," she added, handing it to Karen. "I recommend buying a new copy instead of a used one; it's an excellent resource to have after graduation."

She thumbed through the book. Jan had notes throughout the textbook. She was very thorough.

"What other classes do you have?" Jan asked.

"The rest are all prerequisites. This was the only dietetics class available for the summer quarter," Karen replied.

Chapter 5

"I'm not surprised. There are not —"

Jan and Karen heard a loud knock on Karen's door. "Patty! Get your butt over here!" Ellie yelled. Ellie burst through the door, a huge grin plastered on her face as she looked at Karen and Jan. Patty came running into the room. "What is it?"

"You guys are gonna flip! We've just received an invitation to a fraternity party this Saturday night!"

"Wow!" Patty exclaimed. "How did you do it?"

"I have a few friends," Ellie said with a mischievous smile. "Actually, it was one of the guys I met at the house party the other day. I ran into him in the hallway a few minutes ago. He's an Agger."

"What's an Agger?" Karen asked.

"He belongs to Alpha Gamma Rho; their members are called Aggers," Patty said. "It's an agricultural fraternity."

"I need my fashion consultant to help me pick out a dress, please," Ellie said, looking at Karen.

"Well, Ellie, I liked the Foale and Tuffin we picked out the other day."

With about 48 hours to go before the party, Karen decided to make the Mary Quaint she had seen the other day. With the help of Patty's sewing machine and a quick visit to a fabric store called the Sewing Lounge, she got to work. She found some high-end cotton and linen fabric and a Simplicity dress pattern for a mod dress.

"What do you think?" Karen asked as she modeled her new creation for the girls the next day. "It's the first dress I've ever sewn."

"It looks great," Jan said.

"It's simple and looks good on you," Patty added.

"Do you think it looks OK for a fraternity party because I'm not sure..." Karen asked her friends. "I mean, it's just a simple dress."

"No, it's perfect, Karen," Jan repeated.

They could hear the music and shouts of revelry a block away from Alpha Gamma Rho. Ellie gave them a naughty smile—she was already in the zone. She jabbed the doorbell, and a surprisingly composed figure in a suit coat appeared in the doorway, a stark contrast to the chaos brewing behind him.

"Name?" he asked.

"Richard Peterson invited me. My name is Ellie Cole. This is my sister, Jan, and my friends, Karen and Patty."

Chapter 5

He looked at his clipboard and crossed out her name. "Welcome, ladies," he said, stepping aside. "There are refreshments in the kitchen, and we're going to play games later. I think I saw Rich a few minutes ago in the kitchen."

As usual, the party teemed with a scarcity of women. Ellie immersed herself in the atmosphere—at times, her voice resounded above the crowd as she roared with laughter and shouted. Karen gravitated towards the kitchen, where she chatted and smoked beside the keg. She dominated the boys' attention in the kitchen.

"So, I've been learning about farming," Karen said to the group assembled around the keg. "Before I came here, I thought farmers were backward and uneducated."

The men laughed, and one of them made a comment. "Right, city people always seem to think that. We're pretty well-informed about your world, but you're mainly in the dark about ours."

"What is your degree?" one of them asked.

"I'm studying to be a registered dietitian," Karen replied with a smile. He was tall with a full head of black hair. He smiled back at her.

"What do they do?" he asked back, taking a sip of beer.

"Dietitians work with hospitals and nursing homes to provide optimal nutritional needs for patients. We tell people what to eat to maintain their bodies."

"Interesting."

"You can achieve better health by eating the right foods. For example, as a farmer, your job is physically demanding, and you work long hours. I would recommend carbohydrates, proteins, and lots of water for energy and muscle recovery. I would recommend three meals a day, including a mid-morning snack and an afternoon snack. No junk food."

"Oh," one of them put his head down. "What about drinking?"

"And smoking?" Karen replied, taking a drag from her cigarette and smiling.

The cute one asked, "What about a college student? What is a good diet plan for us?"

"Maintaining brain health is key. Incorporate leafy green vegetables, various berries, healthy nuts such as cashews and almonds, and whole grain breads into your diet. Chicken, fish, and beans are also beneficial for the brain. And no hamburgers."

"How about desserts?" he asked with a smile. "Are there any healthy desserts?"

Karen thought about it for a moment. "Not really, but choosing fruit-based desserts is a better choice."

"Good. Because I love blueberry pie, my mom makes the best."

"So, where are you from?" she asked as more guys came to get beer.

"Goodhue County."

"Where is that?"

"It's about 90 minutes southeast of here on Highway 61. I'm Howard."

"Karen," she replied.

"I've seen you before. I work as a dishwasher at the Dining Center. Where are you from?"

"Rockford, Illinois. It's west of Chicago."

"You're a big city girl," Howard looked back at Karen, smiling.

"Born and raised," she said as she took a sip of liquid courage. "You have a nice smile, Howard," she added, looking into his eyes.

They held each other's gaze for a few seconds before Ellie and Patty burst into the kitchen with a group of guys. "Hey, you!" Ellie said to Karen, hugging her as the guys watched. She pointed to one of the guys and slurred, "Alright, you. I want ta' see how thissis done."

The man stood next to the keg and grabbed the handles. Two men grabbed his legs and lifted them

Chapter 5

over his head. A third man started pumping the keg and stuck the running nozzle in his mouth.

"1, 2, 3, 4, 5, 6..." everyone yelled. After they got to 15, he wiggled his legs, and they let him down. Everyone started to cheer.

"Who's next?" Ellie screamed.

"Who is he?" Patty asked as the girls headed back towards Bailey in the shuttle.

"Just some guy I met," Karen smiled and looked down.

"You two talked for most of the night. So... what's his name?" Patty asked.

"Howard."

"Where is he from?"

"Somewhere south of here, but still in Minnesota. He said something about Highway 61."

"Farmer?"

"He might be," she said, smiling and looking at her heels.

Patty fixed her gaze on Karen, a playful smile dancing on her lips. "You like him, don't you?"

Karen hesitated for a moment; her cheeks tinged with a hint of pink. "Yeah, kind of," she admitted, a shy smile breaking through. "He's… nice."

"The melting point of octadecanoic acid is…" Jan looked at Karen.

Karen looked out the dorm room window at the falling leaves and tried to think. "60 degrees Celsius?"

Jan looked at her and smiled. "No, it's 70 degrees Celsius. The melting point of octadecanoic acid is 70 degrees Celsius. Let's try another question. Can you explain what is meant by the lock and key mechanism?"

"Enzymes have a shape that matches the shape of a substrate, similar to how a key fits a lock," Karen responded.

"And who discovered this theory?" Jan asked.

Karen's face turned blank. "Daniel Koshland?"

"No, Karen. Emil Fischer," she said, closing her book. "You have to study this more."

"I've been studying. Human Chemistry is my most challenging class of the fall semester. How am I going to pass this midterm?"

Chapter 5

"I'll keep quizzing you. I remember taking this midterm last year. Dr. Bryce focuses more on the chemical composition than on the history. That's where I would start. Memorize the chemical compositions in the human body."

"Ugh, okay," Karen said. "Are you hungry, Jan?" *Maybe Howard is working today,* she thought.

"Yes, good idea. Let's go eat."

Jan and Karen were sitting with the other girls from Bailey Hall in the Dining Center. The room had just been decorated with cardboard cutouts of black cats, pumpkins, and witches on brooms. Many of the tables had small pumpkins placed on them. Karen wondered if Howard had helped with the decorations. She had bought a special surprise for him.

As they left, Karen still hadn't caught a glimpse of Howard in the Dining Center. *He must be preoccupied with the dishes today*, she mused. A flutter of butterflies danced in her stomach as she rounded the corner to bus her tray.

He stood there in a white T-shirt, splattered with food stains. The steam in the air made the fabric cling to his skin. His black hair glistened with moisture, which heightened his allure. As she moved closer, her breath quickened; mesmerized, she felt her knees weaken as she stared. Jealousy seared through her heart as Howard chatted with the other Bailey girls, ogling her handsome man.

"Hi Karen!" he said as she got to the front.

With sweaty hands, she set down her tray and handed him a slice of blueberry pie wrapped in plastic wrap. "I found something special for you today," she said, smiling.

"Oh, blueberry!" he exclaimed. "My favorite. Thank you, Karen!"

Her eyes danced with happiness. "You're welcome. See you later," she said, quickly rejoining her friends. They watched with a mix of curiosity and confusion, while Howard kept his gaze fixed on her as she walked away.

"Karen, what are you doing?" Patty asked in a whisper. "Isn't that the frat guy you met at the Aggers' party?"

"Yeah, he told me he likes pie, so I saved him one."

"Wait, I remember him," Patty said. "You two talked most of the night together by the keg, right? Karen, what else do you know about him?"

"Well, not much, I guess," she said. "he's cute, though."

"You shouldn't be baiting him until you know more about him," Jan said.

Chapter 5

"Let me do a little digging," Ellie suggested as she looked at Jan. "My friend Rich probably knows him well enough since he lives in the same fraternity."

"What do babies need that adults don't?" Karen asked, lighting a cigarette.

"Oh, yeah, good question, Karen. Let's add that to the list, too. How many do we have so far?" Michael asked.

"25 questions."

"Perfect!" Michael responded. "That should be enough. There are 20 students in the class, so we'll have five extra questions."

"Should we split the class into two or three groups?" Karen asked.

"I think two groups are fine. Do you want to emcee, or do you want to keep score?"

"Well, I think you're a much better public speaker. I can keep score," Karen replied.

"This is shaping up to be a terrific presentation, Karen! I think we need to go out for pizza and a movie to celebrate," Michael said.

Yes! Karen thought. "Well, I'm free. Where do you want to go?" she asked.

"There's Mama Rosa's in Dinkytown. It's adjacent to the movie theater. It's not as good as New York pizza pie, but it's not bad."

Michael and Karen took the shuttle to Dinkytown. Michael was an attractive man, over six feet tall, with blonde hair and a well-built physique—a real head-turner. During supper, they talked about his baseball scholarship and his role as a center fielder on the Gophers baseball team. He was also a member of the Phi Delta Theta fraternity. A Brooklyn native, he was a passionate Yankees fan, idolizing the iconic center fielder Mickey Mantle.

"When I was 14, my dad bought tickets to a Yankees-Red Sox game. Our seats were right behind third base, and before the game started, Mickey Mantle was signing autographs. He signed the Mickey Mantle jersey I was wearing. During the game, he caught a fly ball in center field and threw out a player at home plate. I knew from that moment I wanted to be a baseball player."

After watching '*Fun in Acapulco,*' the Elvis movie that Karen wanted to see, she caught the shuttle back to Bailey Hall. She arrived at her dorm room around 11 p.m. Since all the lights were out, she quietly slipped off her heels and prepared for bed.

Chapter 5

Patty turned on her bedside lamp. "Where have you been? I was beginning to get worried!"

Even with the dim light, Patty could see Karen's glowing face.

"Okay, I see," she smiled. "Who's the guy?" Patty asked.

Karen ran over to Patty's bunk and sat down, a huge grin on her face. "His name is Michael. We're paired up for a presentation in our Medical Nutrition Therapy class. He asked me out to Mama Rosa's, and then we went to watch *Fun in Acapulco* in Dinkytown."

"Who is he?"

"He plays on the baseball team. He's here on a full scholarship from New York," Karen sighed. "He's tall with blonde hair and very muscular."

"Sounds sexy. How did the date end?" Patty asked, sitting up.

"The movie theater is very close to his fraternity, so he dropped me off at the shuttle stop and kissed me goodnight."

"You bagged another frat guy?"

Karen smiled. "Yes, I did! And he's a good kisser, too."

"He didn't take you home?" Patty asked.

"No, he said he had to get home."

After their date, Karen and Michael became inseparable. Their shared classes led to frequent study sessions together. Sometimes they studied at the library in Minneapolis, other times at the Student Center in Saint Paul, and occasionally in her dorm room at Bailey Hall. Karen's friends enjoyed having Michael around; he was good-looking, and a lot of fun. A week later, Michael asked Karen to go steady.

Michael's last game of the year was a rivalry game against Iowa. Ellie, Patty and Karen got tickets in the bleachers at Delta Field. They agreed to meet up at a sports bar after the game.

"That was fun," Patty said, "but did you understand anything? I know the object of the game is to get to home base by hitting the ball, but how do they know when to switch sides?"

"I found it kind of boring," Ellie said, pouring another glass of beer from the pitcher.

"Michael caught a ball and threw it to home plate. There was a lot of cheering, so I guess he did well," Karen said, taking a sip of her beer.

The television behind them was showing a game between the Yankees and the Detroit Tigers. As Michael

Chapter 5

entered the bar, he walked over to a group of men watching the game.

"Doesn't he see us?" Ellie asked.

"I don't think he knows we're here," Karen replied. She stood up and walked over to him.

"Hi, Michael!" she smiled. "We're sitting in the booth right there," as she pointed to Ellie and Patty.

"Okay, I'll be there in a minute," he said, never taking his eyes away from the television. He barely acknowledged her. Karen walked back to Ellie and Patty with a confused look.

"What's going on? Why isn't he coming over here?" Ellie asked.

"He'll be here in a minute," Karen said.

After 20 minutes, the girls finished the beer and were hungry and tired of waiting, so Karen got up and approached Michael again. He was telling a story about playing stickball on the streets of Brooklyn when he was growing up.

"What kind of toppings do you want on your pizza? And do you want anything to drink?" she asked.

"Just get whatever," he said, not even looking at her and continuing his story. All at once, the guys stood up and cheered. Karen had to step back. She was afraid she might get hit.

Karen marched back to the booth. "He told me to order whatever."

"Maybe we should go," Patty suggested. "I don't think he wants to eat with us."

As they got up to leave, Karen walked over to Michael.

"Michael, you told us to meet you here, and we waited for you, but all you seem to care about are your friends," Karen scolded. "Why did you tell us to meet you here?"

"These are my fraternity brothers. And this is a playoff game," Michael said, looking at Karen for the first time that day. "Stop nagging me."

Just then, a group of girls walked in. He looked over at them and yelled, "Hey, Jennifer!"

"Humph! You have time to wave hello to some floozy, but you won't even look at me."

"Karen, it's not like that."

Karen stomped towards Patty and Ellie. "Come on, we're leaving."

"Karen?" Michael called out as she opened the bar door.

On the shuttle ride back to Saint Paul, the girls opened up about Michael.

Chapter 5

"Karen, I think he cares more about maintaining his reputation on campus than dating you," Patty said. "I didn't want to mention this, but I saw him flirting with a group of girls a couple of weeks ago."

Ellie added, "Yeah, I had a run-in with him, too. He started hitting on me on my bed one night when all of us were drunk. He made me feel very uncomfortable."

"Why didn't you tell me that?" Karen stared at Ellie. "I thought you were my friend?"

Ellie put her hand on Karen's. "I am your friend, Karen. I told my sister, and we thought it best to stay quiet. But today made me realize that he is not serious. He's just having fun."

"This is all my fault. I should've been more serious about the relationship," Karen said, shaking her head. "I really like him. And he's also in many of my classes. I have to see him all the time!"

"You saw his true colors today, and you still like him?" Ellie asked, "If you ask me, I think you like the idea of him."

As the bus stopped in front of Bailey Hall, the three girls jumped out.

"Karen let's see what he does next," Patty said as they signed into the dorm. "He will either be apologetic or nonchalant about the sports bar incident."

Karen flipped through her Human Chemistry final exam. There was an excessive amount of red ink, especially in the chemical composition section. *I'm better than this*, she thought.

The teacher's assistant announced, "Once you are done reviewing your final, please turn it in to me. I will check your name off the list. You are forbidden to take your final exam outside of this room."

The failing grade on her exam shattered Karen's heart. She returned the test and staggered from the room, her steps heavy and aimless as she wandered toward Bailey, until the undeniable truth finally dawned: she'd failed a crucial dietetics course.

A profound darkness cloaked Bailey Hall, reflecting the sentiment felt around the world in the wake of yesterday's news. She checked in and watched the latest updates from the lobby. They had identified the Kennedy assassin as Lee Harvey Oswald and declared Monday a National Day of Mourning. Though tempted to sit and join her dormmates, she yearned for solitude after the test. Patty had already left for Thanksgiving, and Ellie and Jan were driving home after lunch.

She sank onto her bed; her gaze fixed on the ceiling as a silent question echoed in the empty room: *What am I going to do?* This course was the cornerstone of the dietetics program. A single tear escaped, then another, until the salty dampness blurred her vision.

"You're kidding, an F? You told me you had this down, Karen."

"We studied this so many times, Jan," Karen said, shaking her head. "I just don't understand how I could do this badly. After the test, I expected to score at least 80%, if not higher. Receiving 64% was a shock. I feel that I have no choice but to retake the class. An F in one of my critical courses for my major will significantly lower my GPA."

"You're right about that," Jan said. "Employers look at that. However, if you retake the course, the F will still appear on your transcript, unfortunately. You don't get the F removed even if you improve the grade. It is part of your GPA now."

"Ugh," Karen sighed.

"No, not this year, Grandpa," Karen said.

"You missed last Thanksgiving, too, but this... this year is different. Karen, the world's been traumatized by this Godless act, and everyone is struggling to make sense of it. We need to be together now. Come home."

"Grandpa, I've got a lot on my mind," Karen sighed. "I failed my Human Chemistry course."

"The one you were having difficulties with?"

"Yes, Grandpa, that one," Karen replied.

"What are you going to do?" he asked.

"I don't know yet. Jan tells me that the grade is on my permanent record."

"Oh, I see," Grandpa replied. "Choosing what you want to do for the rest of your life is difficult and requires a lot of thought and contemplation. Have you prayed about it?"

"No, I should do that," Karen replied.

"Before studying theology, I realized my strength in public speaking. I also had a deep belief in God as my savior. In my opinion, it's essential to find something you excel at and something you truly believe in."

Chapter 5

He always knew what to say.

"Is this a sign?" he continued. "Maybe you weren't meant to leave Concordia after all."

"Grandpa, I'm not moving back to Morehead."

"I think it's important for you to come home, dear. This would be a great opportunity for you to reconnect with your parents and hear their thoughts. Just take a bus and come home."

"Okay, Grandpa."

"Good. I look forward to seeing you on Thursday morning for church."

After she hung up, she realized the drama with Olga would be too much right now. She needed time to herself.

Monday dawned, cloaked in a welcome hush. Bailey Hall, typically abuzz with girls preparing for the day, now echoed with an unsettling quiet. She lingered, letting the deep stillness seep into her bones. A luxurious, steamy shower followed, the hot spray hers alone, with no urgency imposed by a waiting line. Walking back to her room, her footsteps were the only sound. *Am I truly the only one left?* As she got ready, an insistent grumble in her stomach beckoned her towards the Dining Center.

She arrived just before 10:30 a.m., as the chefs were transitioning from breakfast to lunch. She glanced at the pie options and noticed that there was no blueberry pie available today. *Just in case*, she thought. She picked up a cherry pie and headed to the checkout.

The room held a scattering of Middle Eastern and Asian students, but none of the familiar faces from Bailey Hall. She chose a secluded table and began eating her breakfast.

"May I join you?" Howard asked.

Karen looked up with an expression of happy surprise. "What are you doing here?" she asked.

"I have to work until Tuesday night," Howard said. "The whole school is closing down for the Kennedy funeral this afternoon, so I only have to work through lunch. Why are you here? I was surprised to see you." He set down his half-eaten breakfast and took a seat across from Karen.

"I don't want to go home," Karen said, looking down at her tray.

"Why not? Picture this..." Howard said, raising his hand. "A table with turkey, stuffing, green-bean casserole, cranberry sauce, and blueberry pie for dessert. That's enough reason for me to go home, even if I was in... Chicago?"

Karen chuckled at his playful intentions. "Rockford."

Chapter 5

"That's right. Rockford."

"Well, the food sounds delicious, but the company does not. There's a lot of... drama with my family."

"Oh, I see. Sorry to hear that," he said, biting his toast.

"Also, I need some time alone. I failed a very important course for my dietetics major. I need to rethink where I'm heading."

"Do you think you need to change career paths?" he asked. "I mean, I think you'd make a great dietitian."

Karen smiled. "That's sweet, thank you. But failing Human Chemistry is a blow to my degree."

"What's your dream?" Howard asked.

"Well, my dream was to become a dietitian, or so I thought."

"What are you good at?" Howard asked, taking a bite of pancakes.

"Well," Karen thought for a moment. "I was a Sunday school teacher for years. I also tutored other students at school. And I'm good at getting into trouble," she said, smiling.

"Maybe that's your dream," he said.

"Getting into trouble?" Karen smiled.

"No, teaching children," Howard said. "I could see that about you."

Chapter 5

Howard paused for a moment. "I haven't shared this with anyone. I have a dream: I want to start a cattle business on my dad's farm."

"Why?" Karen asked. "I mean, why a cattle farm?

"I see an opportunity here. If I sell meat directly to small businesses and individuals, I could make significantly more money than if I were to sell it to slaughterhouses. I have a great location, just north of Rochester, along with the education and resources to do this properly. However, I need someone to help me market this to customers, as sales is not my strong suit."

"Wow. You've put a lot of thought into this."

"I've even written up a business proposal."

Karen finished her French toast, took a sip of cranberry juice, and then remarked, "Impressive. It sounds like a fantastic idea."

Howard wiped his mouth with a napkin. "I think it's wise for you to stay on campus this week. This is a critical moment in your life; this decision will shape your future. You need time to reflect away from friends and family, especially if there are problems at home."

Finally, she thought, *someone who supports my decision.*

"I have to get to work now, but I really enjoyed our conversation," Howard said as he stood up. "I hope you have a nice Thanksgiving, Karen."

"Oh, wait!" She remembered the pie. "This is for you. There were no blueberry pies today."

Howard's eyes smiled as he placed the cherry pie on his tray. "While blueberry is my favorite, any pie you give me is a close second. Thanks, Karen. Have a good week," he said, heading over to the dishwashing area.

The main library in Dinkytown proved to be a wise choice. They offered a vast array of resources tailored to every major at the university. It served as the perfect launchpad for her research.

After a few hours of contemplation, Karen narrowed her choices down to two potential majors: fashion merchandising or elementary education. Both paths required her to attend summer school in her junior and senior years to catch up, as they were Bachelor of Science degrees.

She was drawn to the idea of buying and selling clothing for boutiques, finding the fashion industry exciting and easy to grasp. However, she realized that she lacked the necessary business acumen to succeed. To thrive in this field, she needed to focus on business classes, especially in areas such as retail operations and negotiation skills.

Chapter 5

She also liked the idea of teaching children in an elementary school setting. She had been doing this for years at her church. It brought her joy to see her young students learning stories about Jesus; she was sure this field would bring her happiness in her career. *It's not a job if you enjoy it*, she thought.

On Tuesday, she visited each of the colleges. Since most students were home for the Thanksgiving holiday, she had the opportunity to speak with a career consultant from both schools.

"I wish you had come home," Olga said. "This is the second Thanksgiving you've missed."

"I understand. However, having time to myself has allowed me to reflect on my future."

"Well, did you make any decisions?" she asked.

"Yes, I've decided," Karen said. "I'm going to pursue a Bachelor of Science in elementary education."

"She decided to pursue a degree in elementary education," Karen heard Olga say to her family. In the background, the sounds of Thanksgiving dinner filled the air as silverware clinked against her mom's fine china.

"Praise the Lord. Great choice," she heard her grandfather say.

"Unfortunately, it's located on the West Bank. I will have to leave Bailey Hall and my friends because the school is too far away. The career consultant is looking for openings in a West Bank dormitory. The College of Education is situated in Burton Hall, which was formerly the library at the turn of the century. Burton Hall is the oldest building at the University of Minnesota. It features a grand wooden staircase and marble statues on the exterior, resembling a Greek temple!"

By the following Monday, the College of Education's career consultant secured her enrollment in several 200-level courses for the winter quarter. Although her move to Comstock Hall was confirmed, it wouldn't take place until next fall, necessitating her continued residence at Bailey Hall and reliance on the shuttle service for the winter and spring quarters.

"Karen, I suggest you ask Pi Beta Phi if you can live there over the summer," the consultant suggested. "It's within walking distance of Burton Hall, and they have been known to take in non-sorority students over the summer."

Chapter 5

"You're leaving me?" Ellie said, putting her fork down. Sadness was written on her face. "Who's gonna be my fashion consultant?"

"Well, it's not until the end of the spring quarter," Karen said. "I'm going to move to Pi Beta Phi after finals."

"How did you manage that?" another girl asked, "you're not a Pi Phi?"

"The Pi Phi house allows students to stay over the summer if there are empty rooms available. I spoke with the chapter president yesterday, and she told me I could move in right after finals. I even had the opportunity to check out my room!"

"We will miss eating dinner with you, Karen," one of the Bailey girls said. A few other girls agreed.

"Well, at least you'll be closer to Michael, living on the West Bank. How is that going? He's quite a catch," another said.

"Something feels off. When I mentioned that I was changing my major and leaving dietetics, his response felt hollow, and he started talking about how all these baseball scouts were watching him play. It's becoming clear to me that his priorities lie with the career and himself, not our relationship."

The weekend before Spring Jam, Alpha Gamma Rho hosted "Aggie Day," an annual fundraiser that supported 4-H Clubs. This community-wide event featured a pie-eating contest, wheelbarrow races, an archery contest, and a variety of other games. Over the years, it became so popular that the University of Minnesota allowed Alpha Gamma Rho to use The Lawn for the event. The highlight of the day was the auction, where members of Alpha Gamma Rho auctioned themselves off for a date on the steps of the SPSC.

Karen and Michael had planned to meet up at the event. However, when she arrived with the girls, she spotted Michael surrounded by his fraternity brothers, their camaraderie evident as they laughed and joked while shooting bows and arrows. Karen stared, feeling a pang of jealousy and disappointment.

"Why don't you hang out with us today, Karen?" Ellie asked.

"Yeah, you're leaving soon, and we won't get to see you anymore," Patty added.

Karen smiled at her friends.

Chapter 5

Howard judged the hula hoop contest, and the girls enjoyed competing against one another. Jan surprised everyone with her skills, going for over 10 minutes.

"I'm truly impressed by the talented women here. I can't even hula hoop for 15 seconds, but some of you managed to go for over 15 minutes!" Howard announced over the PA system. "Congratulations to Ruth Campbell from South Saint Paul, who outlasted the competition with an impressive time of 17 minutes and 34 seconds." The other participants and spectators applauded as Ruth came up to accept her trophy.

As her friends went to check out other events, Karen stayed behind and helped pick up hula hoops.

"Thanks for your help, Karen!" Howard said.

Karen beamed at Howard. "No problem. How have you been?"

"Classes have been challenging this quarter. Doctor George's Plant Chemistry course has been difficult."

"Chemistry is not one of my favorite subjects either," Karen said as she placed hula hoops in the carrier.

"Yes, I remember discussing it over breakfast last fall. What did you decide to do?"

"After researching and talking with my friends and my grandfather, I changed my major to Elementary Education."

"Well, I think you made a great choice!" he said as they picked up more hula hoops.

"Commuting daily between Burton Hall on the West Bank and Bailey has been tough. I'll be happy when I move to Pi Beta Phi on the West Bank this summer."

"Wait, you're a Pi Phi?" Howard said, stopping cold and looking at her. "Congratulations!"

"No," Karen said. "I'm just living there over the summer quarter," Karen said in a reflective tone. "I'm gonna miss my friends in Bailey."

Meanwhile, across The Lawn, Ellie was helping her friend Rich set up the wheelbarrow races.

"How well do you know Howard?" Ellie asked.

"Pretty well. He's one of my closest friends in the fraternity," Rich said, lining up wheelbarrows before the race's starting line.

"Tell me about him," she asked.

"He grew up on a second-generation dairy and corn farm near Lake City, Minnesota. Like me, he attended a small one-room schoolhouse until high school. His best friend, Dick, lived just across the road. After graduating, Dick chose to pursue a religious path and is now a third-year seminary student at Concordia in Saint Paul. Howard is feeling a little bummed out since Dick's family lost their farm. He thought they would be neighbors after he got his degree. Howard is always

Chapter 5

looking for ways to innovate and improve his family's farm. His drip irrigation experiments have even made national news!"

"So, after graduation, what is Howard doing?"

"He made a deal with his parents – they would pay for four years of college if he took over the family farm. So, after graduation, I imagine he's moving back to Lake City," Rich said. "Why do you ask?"

"I'm asking for a friend," she said, helping him line up wheelbarrows. "When does the race start?"

"The girls' race will start in a few minutes. Are you and your sister competing?" Rich asked.

"She doesn't like this kind of thing. But I'm sure Karen or Patty will be on my team!" she replied.

"Ellie, I've got to go check-in. I'll see you at the finish line. Good luck!" he called over his shoulder as he walked off.

A wave of anticipation rippled through the crowd as the emcee announced, "Ladies, this year's auction features five of our most charming Aggers!" He swept a hand towards his fraternity brothers, a group of five men, half-dressed in Levis and classic cowboy boots. The women erupted in a frenzy of enthusiastic cheers.

"Our first Agger is a junior from Lake City, Minnesota. He likes fast cars, Gopher football, and blueberry pie. Meet Howard Boatman."

Howard stepped to the front of the stage as the girls yelled, "Turn around! Turn around!" Howard twirled around and smiled at the crowd. The girls approved.

"Well, who wants to go on a date with this handsome Agger? The bidding starts at five dollars."

Karen yelled, "Five dollars!" as the emcee pointed at her and confirmed the bid. Howard smiled at her. The bidding quickly escalated to $20 within seconds. Karen felt jealous as two more girls engaged in a bidding war.

"Ladies, remember that all proceeds help the 4-H Club. Don't be shy."

The winning bid was $25. An older woman took the stage and posed for a picture next to Howard.

She's not Howard's type, Karen thought to herself. *She looks like a bimbo.*

After the auction, the girls ate dinner at the Dining Center.

"That was so much fun," Patty said.

"You're just happy because you and Ellie won the wheelbarrow race," Karen responded.

Chapter 5

"Karen," Ellie commenced, her gaze skirting her friend's eyes for a moment as she speared a piece of food on her fork rather than eating it. "Rich and I talked about Howard this afternoon. He's... returning to his family farm after school. He's a farmer." The fork clattered softly onto her plate, and she released a small, regretful sigh. "I'm so sorry to break this news. I know how much he meant to you."

"He's much too cute to be a farmer," Patty responded, touching Karen's arm. "I'm sorry, too."

"I told him today I was moving to the West Bank after spring quarter." Karen sighed. "You know, he's out of my league; I could only dream of a guy like that. Oh well, at least I got to see him topless!"

"Yeah, he's great eye candy!" Ellie added.

Karen dedicated most of her Sunday to studying for her final exam in Applied Psychology in the Classroom. It was an unusually hot day for late May, so she opened the window in her bedroom to let in some fresh air. Before heading out for dinner, she made her weekly phone call to her grandfather.

"Are you looking forward to moving to Minneapolis?" he asked.

"I will miss my roommate Patty and my friends Ellie and Jan, but walking to Burton Hall will be nice instead of commuting for 30 minutes."

"How do you like the classes?"

"These courses are easier than the dietitian ones. But this applied psychology class is pretty confusing sometimes."

"When is that final?" he asked.

"Monday afternoon. It's my first one."

"Pray about it, and best of luck. In Rockford news, the downtown lighting project has finally been completed. Next weekend is the grand opening. Miss Illinois and Miss Wisconsin will be present to flip the switch and turn on the neon lights."

"Wow, they finally got that done!" Karen replied. "They were working on that when I left years ago."

At supper, most of the girls, including Karen, were tired from studying all day. Most of the chit-chat revolved around classes and summer vacation.

Howard was working in the dishwashing area as Karen and her friends left the Dining Center. Karen thought back to the auction and how she had seen him topless. The memory still made her weak in the knees.

"Sorry, Howard, they were all out of blueberry pie today," Karen said as she got to the front of the line.

His eyes found hers, then ricocheted off, looking down at the bussed trays. His hand tipped over a glass. Karen watched him, raising a perplexed eyebrow as she stood there, a cherry pie in her hand.

"So, uh, dinner and a movie?" he stammered, the words tumbling out.

Karen's eyes widened, caught completely off guard, as she found herself saying, "Yes."

Ellie silently mouthed, "What!?" to Patty. The three of them stared at Howard and Karen.

Howard's face lit up. "Great! When would you like to go?"

"Umm, well, I'm done with finals on Wednesday afternoon. How about you?"

"My last final is on Thursday afternoon. How about we go out on Thursday night to celebrate? I'll pick you up at Bailey Hall around 5 p.m."

"Okay," she replied, her eyes beaming.

"I'll see you then! And thank you," he said awkwardly, turning his attention back to the dirty dishes.

Karen started walking towards her friends, who were waiting with their mouths agape. The four of them walked out of the Dining Center, unsure of what to say.

Chapter 5

"Karen?" Patty asked.

"Look. Michael is self-centered and clearly not invested in our relationship. Did you see how he was showboating during Aggie Day? The way he flaunted himself was not only embarrassing but childish."

"But you need to end it with Michael before you go out with someone else," Jan said. "Even if you don't like him anymore, that's not fair to Michael."

"Did you see how nervous Howard was?" Patty said. "Karen, I think he's carrying a torch for you."

"Karen, listen to me," Ellie said, stopping in her tracks and looking directly into Karen's eyes. "I spoke with his friend Rich during Aggie Day. Do you remember what I told you just now? Are you prepared to become a farmer's wife? Think about it—your days will likely revolve around cooking meals, cleaning the farmhouse, and caring for a large family. You deserve more than a life focused solely on domestic duties. "

"Ellie, geez, it's just a date. He didn't propose to me." Karen looked down and smiled.

But the girls had seen that look in Karen's eyes before.

To her delight, Karen received three As and one B for the quarter, including a B in Applied Psychology in the Classroom, surpassing her expectations. Ellie let her borrow the Pierre Cardin dress for her date with Howard. Howard arrived promptly at 5 p.m., and Karen ran downstairs to meet him. He looked handsome in a black suit and tie, holding a bouquet in his left hand.

"Wow! You looked incredible, Karen," Howard said, "these are for you," and handed her the flowers.

"Thank you, they're beautiful!" Karen replied, smiling at Howard. She asked the desk to bring them up to her room.

"I've arranged a double date with one of my fraternity brothers," he announced as they walked towards the parking area. In the distance, a small cluster of students admired a black 1931 Model A coupe. A symbol of a bygone era, it was a striking contrast to the modern campus landscape. Its black paint gleamed like polished obsidian under the late-afternoon sun, while the open rumble seat lured them, a perfect invitation to an open-air adventure.

As they approached, he introduced his fraternity brother, Paul, and his date, Diane. From the driver's seat, Paul enjoyed entertaining the crowd with the Model A's classic 'ah-oo-ga' horn, each blast drawing cheers and laughs from the onlookers. Howard and

Karen settled into the rumble seat as the coupe coughed, then roared to vibrant life.

"What a great car! I remember these cars when I was little. I've never ridden in one," Karen replied.

"Neither have I," Diane replied. "It's so unique and different."

They made their way over to Dinkytown, the center of attention on the road. It was a beautiful May night, perfect for a ride in a convertible.

Securing a prime spot at the drive-in, they parked their eye-catching Model A and ordered cheeseburgers and chocolate shakes, commanding the attention of the entire restaurant. The two couples had a great time chatting about finals, their dreams for the future, and what they wanted out of life. It was great to get to know each other better in such a chilled atmosphere. As the date wore on, Howard began to relax, letting go of his nervousness and showing off his fun side.

The clock struck 7 p.m. as they took their seats for *Dr. Zhivago*. As the film lumbered onward, Howard's arm draped around Karen, creating an immediate, comforting warmth. A gentle serenity blossomed within her chest, and her head, without conscious thought, yielded to the curve of his shoulder. His arms

Chapter 5

gave her a sense of profound tranquility, a peace she had never known in all her 22 years.

Karen was the first to be dropped off after the movie. Howard walked her back to Bailey Hall.

"That was a longer movie than I thought," Howard said.

"The movie was slow to get going," Karen added.

Karen stopped in front of the dorm. "Well, I had a delightful time tonight. Thank you again for the flowers."

Howard's smile lit up his face. *He has such a beautiful smile. No wonder everyone likes him*, she thought. His approach sent a delicious shiver through her, her heart a frantic little bird in her ribs. The soft brush of his lips against hers stole the air from her lungs, freezing the moment. A raw, powerful longing had always hung between them, something that did not have a voice until now. This wasn't John, Michael, or any other man. No, this was substantial, momentous, and real. When he finally pulled away, their eyes met, almost deer-like in their wide, stunned vulnerability, as the realization of what just happened still processed in their minds.

"Well, good night," Howard's voice quivered, the gravity of the moment still clinging to his gaze. He stared just a little too long and finally turned away, leaving Karen's mouth agape and her breath snagged in her throat. A hollow ache gripped her as he rounded the corner.

Chapter 6

Howard stumbled back towards the Model A, his heart a frantic drum against his chest, his hands slick with sweat. His senses were going haywire, each blade of grass unnaturally sharp beneath his feet, and the faraway murmur of conversation seemed to swell and diminish. *That was some kiss!*

Diane stepped out as Howard approached to open the rumble seat. "Karen made it back?" she asked, looking at him. All the color had drained from his face. "Whoa, are you okay?"

Howard looked Diane dead in the eye and gave her a confused look. "Yeah, I'm okay," he replied in a shaky voice. Paul looked at Howard.

"You look like you've seen a ghost," he said.

Howard climbed into the rumble seat, and Diane looked back at him. "You're sweating, and you look like you're a million miles away. What happened?"

"I just kissed Karen goodnight," he replied, "then I started walking towards the car."

"Did you eat something bad? Are you sick to your stomach?" Paul asked.

Diane slapped him on the arm. "Paul, stop! How romantic!" Diane cooed, looking at Paul. "How come you never kiss me like that?"

After dropping off Diane and returning the Model A, Howard and Paul headed to the fraternity. A few of the guys were hanging out in the common room, studying for their finals.

"Hey, Howard, how did the date go?"

"I think it went pretty well," he replied.

"That's great!"

"You've been looking forward to this date for a few days," another remarked.

"I didn't think she would say yes when I asked her out, but I felt I had to try since she's leaving for the West Bank next week. She's out of my league, so I knew I needed to do something special to impress her. It was Paul's idea to rent a Model A with a rumble seat."

"You're welcome," Paul said.

"Isn't she one of Ellie Cole's friends? Man, those girls are showstoppers. How did you get a date with her?" one asked.

Chapter 6

"I heard Karen is dating one of the varsity baseball players from New York," another replied. "Are you sure she's free?"

"I didn't know that," Howard said.

"So, if the date went well, are you going to ask her out again?" someone asked.

Howard stopped cold. "I should do it before she leaves for the West Bank. I might not get another chance!"

Howard stared at the ceiling, the next day's final shift at the Dining Center a heavy weight on his mind. A knot tightened in his stomach, his heart hammering against his ribs at the thought of her leaving before he had another chance to ask her out.

He arrived at the Dining Center thirty minutes before his shift was set to begin. As he walked through the dining area, he hoped to spot Karen. Although a few of the Bailey girls were present, Karen was not among them. Howard sighed and proceeded to the back, where he put on his apron and started his shift.

Just as Howard's hopes began to dwindle, Karen and her friends approached to bus their trays. A spark of joy ignited in his chest as he watched Karen approach. All of her friends exchanged mischievous smiles.

"Hello, ladies. How are you this evening?" Howard's heart raced as he tried to decipher their expressions.

"Hi, Howard!" Karen said when she reached the front of the line. "A few of us are going to the casino party tonight at the Student Center. Would you like to join us?"

"Yes!" he replied without even thinking about it.

Karen's face lit up. "Great! Can't wait to see you there!" She turned on her heels and joined her friends. Howard looked over and saw that they were all staring at the two of them talking.

After finishing his shift, Howard stopped by his fraternity to take a quick shower and made his way to the casino party. When he arrived, he presented his student ID at the entrance and received $500 in fake currency. The atmosphere buzzed with energy; the air was thick with smoke and laughter, punctuated by the occasional whoop of joy from winners celebrating their luck at the tables. He spotted Karen and Patty sitting at a table by the buffet. Karen was wearing a new red dress and matching red heels.

"May I join you?" he asked. At the sound of his voice, Karen's eyes sparkled as she met Howard's gaze.

Chapter 6

"Only if you have some casino money!" Patty said matter-of-factly and taking a drag from her cigarette. "We are all out."

"Ahh, you lost all your money?" Howard replied, sitting down.

"On the roulette wheel. A few minutes ago, I put all of it on black."

"How about you, Karen? Did you lose all your money as well?" Howard asked.

"No, I still have some left. I don't know how to play any of these games," Karen said. "Oh, this is my roommate, Patty."

"Yes, I remember seeing you a couple of times. So, you two are roommates?"

"Well, until this weekend, Ellie is moving in with me," Patty said, looking at Karen. "I want to thank you for the flowers, Howard. They brightened up the room."

"Well, they were for Karen," he said, confused.

"Yes, but I enjoyed them too!" she smiled at Howard. "Alright, let's go play some more games! Karen, I'll teach you how to play roulette. Perhaps Howard would be kind enough to lend us some money?" She clasped her hands together in a prayer position and gave Howard a sorrowful look.

Karen watched in disbelief as her birthday number, 22, won not once, but twice! She pumped a fist in the air as Patty nudged Howard. While Karen joined the chorus of excited shouts, cheering for their numbers, Patty and Howard enjoyed the show, perfectly content to watch instead of play.

"You know, Karen is a very peaceful sleeper," Patty said to Howard. "She sleeps like a little angel." Patty looked at Howard and added, "However, she struggles with insecurities in her relationships because of her childhood."

He decided to ask. "Is she dating anyone right now?" and met Patty's gaze.

"I'm not sure," Patty replied with a sly grin. "She was dating Michael, but I don't think it's serious anymore. I believe there's someone else involved."

"I see," he smiled.

After Karen blew all her winnings, the three of them headed back to Bailey Hall.

"Well, thank you, girls, for a delightful evening."

"What's your hurry?" Patty asked.

"It's late, and I should be getting back to the fraternity," he replied. "Besides, don't you have a curfew at midnight?"

"Oh, I didn't realize it was so late," Patty said, looking at the clock on the lobby wall. "Well, I'll see you up in the room, Karen."

Chapter 6

"It's nice to see you again, Patty," Howard said. With that, Patty turned and began to ascend the steps to the third floor.

They watched Patty as she walked away. "I'm really going to miss her. She's my best friend," Karen said.

"Well, it's not like you're changing schools," Howard replied. "I'm sure you'll see her again."

"Oh, for sure!"

Howard took a deep breath. "I enjoyed our date the other night," he said.

"Me too!"

"So, before I head back to Lake City, would you like to go out to dinner with me?"

"I would love to," she replied with a warm smile and a twinkle in her eye.

"Great! Let's meet tomorrow night at 6 o'clock right here."

"Okay," she replied. Since there were many people coming and going, he quickly kissed her on the cheek and headed out the door.

The next day, Howard went through everything in his mind.

Cleaned and ironed shirts—check. Reservations—check. Money— he checked his wallet. He had enough for two sodas at the shop, but not for an Italian dinner date.

"Think, Howard," he said aloud. He could ask one of his fraternity brothers, but most had already left for the summer. Then he remembered that his dad had given him an emergency credit card. He reached into his wallet and took out the American Express card. *This is kind of an emergency*, he thought. *But I should ask for permission to use this.*

This meant calling his mother since his dad would be working in the field. It also meant calling the party line, and he didn't want to share with everyone that he needed money for a date. But he had no choice.

"Hi, I am looking for Evelyn Boatman," he asked the party line.

"Is this little Howard? How is college going?" Mrs. Forthright was always the first on the line when it rang.

Howard recognized the voice. "It's going well, Mrs. Forthright."

"Are you coming home this summer?" she asked.

"Yes, I'll be there next week," he replied.

"Hello, Howard! Nice to hear your voice," said another woman. "How are things in the Cities?"

"Just fine," he replied.

Chapter 6

"Howard, is that you?" his mother asked.

"Mom, you picked up! How are you?"

"Is everything okay? Why are you calling on a weekday afternoon?"

"I need permission to use the emergency credit card Dad gave me," he asked.

"What's wrong, dear?"

"Oh, nothing's wrong. I just need to use the credit card," he asked again.

"Why? Are you in trouble?"

Howard sighed. "I have a date, and I don't have enough money to pay for it. I will pay you back next week when I get home."

"Oh, all right. But you should tell your father."

"The date is tonight. And I won't get to talk to him before the date!?"

"Well, I'll tell him over supper."

"During high school, I had to drive to school or have my dad drop me off at the bus stop on the outskirts of town," Howard said as the light turned green. His Beetle bounced to life with its quirky doof-doof-doof sound while picking up speed.

"We didn't have school buses in town. We always walked to school," Karen said. "My elementary school was only two blocks away, but the high school was a mile away. It took about 20 minutes to walk to West Rockford."

They pulled into the parking lot at Vescio's and headed inside.

"Boatman—reservation for two," Howard told the server, who grabbed a couple of menus and seated them by a window overlooking the Mississippi River.

"So, tell me more about yourself," Howard asked.

"Well, what do you want to know?" she said, opening the menu.

"What was your childhood like?" he asked, taking a sip of water.

"My parents were quite strict, coming from traditional backgrounds. My grandfather is a Lutheran pastor at a church south of Rockford, which meant that my life revolved around the church. When I was 10, I began teaching Sunday school for preschool children. I played the piano and sang, and I also played the viola for several years. I was 1st viola for the West Rockford Orchestra during my junior and senior years."

"Wow!" Howard's face cringed. "What's a viola?"

Karen giggled. "It's a little larger than a violin, producing a deeper and richer sound."

Chapter 6

One of the things that made Vescio's a beloved Italian restaurant is its fantastic waitstaff. All the servers were born and raised in Italy and truly knew their stuff when it came to Italian cuisine and wine. Most customers would simply ask for ideas with meat or seafood, and the waiters would create a wonderful dining experience just for them. A few minutes after choosing their entrees, their waiter returned with a bottle of *Montepulciano d'Abruzzo.*

"Did you have any brothers or sisters?" Howard asked as he took a sip of wine.

Karen took a deep breath. "No, I was an only child," she said, casting a guilty glance at Howard and taking a long drink of water. Howard saw that Karen looked worried. *This might be what Patty meant when she said that Karen had a hard childhood.* He decided to steer the conversation in a different direction as the waiter returned with some *bruschetta* and *arancini. Your timing couldn't be better*, he thought.

After taking a couple of bites, Karen asked, "So, Howard, how about you? Tell me about yourself."

"It's not very exciting. I grew up on a farm. As a child, I would wake up every morning at 4 a.m. to milk cows, collect eggs, feed the chickens and pigs, and clean the barn before heading to school. When I was older, I also worked in the fields after school. My dad and I grew corn and soybeans on 85 acres. During the planting and harvest seasons in May and October, we were extremely busy. I often had to miss school for several days to help."

"You woke up at 4 a.m. every day?" she asked, sipping the wine. "That's a lot of responsibility for a young kid."

"Yes," he replied.

"What did you do for fun?" she asked. "Didn't you have friends you could play with?"

"My best friend, Dick, lived across the road. We also walked to the schoolhouse together during grade school," he said. He was starting to feel uncomfortable with all these questions.

"Schoolhouse?" Karen asked.

"We had a one-room country schoolhouse," he said, taking a sip of water. "There were about 20 kids, all aged between 5 and 15."

"So, no grades? Five-year-olds would be learning next to 15-year-olds? That doesn't make any sense?"

"Well, it worked," he smiled, reflecting on his childhood.

"So, your brothers and sisters went to the schoolhouse, too?"

"I didn't have any."

Karen looked at Howard for a moment. "It's lonely, growing up by yourself, isn't it?"

"Yes."

Why such curt answers? she thought. "I was lucky, I guess," Karen finally said. "I had lots of girlfriends. We would talk and play games together. But my parents were so strict, Howard. When I entered high school, I had a rebellious streak. My friends and I would take my parents' car to Wisconsin and drink every weekend. I couldn't wait to get far away from Rockford," she said, popping an *arancini* in her mouth. "How about you? Were your parents strict? Did you wanna get away from the farm?"

"Yes."

Karen looked outside the window for inspiration. "How about girlfriends? Did you have any girlfriends in high school or college?"

"Yes, Mary."

"Tell me about her," she said, taking another sip of wine.

"Well, there isn't much to say," he said.

"Where did you meet?"

"At high school."

"How long did you date for?"

"Three years."

Chapter 6

Finally, the food arrived. Karen continued with the questions.

"What are your mother and father like?" she asked.

"My mother and I do exactly as we are told."

Karen's hand, halfway to her mouth with a bite of eggplant parmesan, froze, her left eyebrow raised. They ate dinner in silence.

"How was your meal?" the waiter asked a few minutes later.

"It tasted delicious. And the wine was perfect," Karen replied.

"*Ottimo*!" he replied in an Italian accent as he picked up the plates. "I've ordered a lovely tiramisu for two, perfect for a first date," he winked at Karen as he walked away.

"And two coffees, please," Howard called after him.

Howard looked back at Karen, who was looking outside the window again.

"What's wrong?" he asked.

She looked at him, confused, and blurted out, "Did I say something to upset you?"

"No."

"Then why won't you tell me anything about yourself?"

Howard was confused. *I've answered all her questions*, he thought.

"Howard, you need to be open with me. Tell me how you feel," Karen said, shaking her head. "I still don't know anything about you. Do you have any dreams besides opening a cattle farm? What's an important moment that you remember from your childhood?"

Howard thought for a moment. "Well, one Christmas my father gave me a tractor."

"And how did you feel after he gave you that tractor?" she quizzed.

"Fine. It was just the tractor, no implements," he said.

Karen shut her eyes and sighed. "Were you happy when you got the tractor?"

"Sure. I guess."

The waiter arrived with the tiramisu and the coffee. They ate in silence.

"On Monday morning, I have to start helping on the farm for the summer," he said, struggling to think of something to say.

"Well, the summer quarter starts on Monday. This weekend I'm moving to the sorority. The only break I will get is for the Fourth of July week."

Chapter 6

As the bill arrived, Howard produced his dad's gleaming American Express card. Karen's glance sharpened, captivated by the casual yet undeniable display of his family's prosperity.'

Driving back to Bailey Hall in the Beetle, Howard knew the relationship was in trouble, especially with three long months of summer ahead and her ex-boyfriend, a baseball player, still in the picture. Crossing the bridge, inspiration struck.

He swallowed hard, the breath hitching in his chest before the words came tumbling out. "Would you like to come to the farm during your Fourth of July break?"

Karen scoffed. "Go to your farm," she said. "And do what?"

"Well," he said, "there are lots of things we can do. We can go to the A&W drive-in. We can watch the Fourth of July fireworks. I can introduce you to my parents and Dick."

"I've never been on a farm in my life," she said.

"There are lots of farm animals," Howard said with a smile. "You told me when we first met that you were concerned about what you eat. There are lots of things to learn about where your food comes from."

Karen looked at Howard. "You remember the day we met?"

"Of course I do!" he said, looking back at her. "It was during the summer of my internship at the fraternity."

Karen hesitated with a gentle pause. "I was planning to visit my family in Rockford for the Fourth—I haven't seen them in months—but this sounds more interesting," she said, gazing thoughtfully out the Beetle's passenger window. "Okay, I'll talk to my grandfather and postpone my trip. I'll need your parents' phone number so I can call you."

Chapter 7

In the summer of 1964, the United States experienced a notable rise in demonstrations and rallies advocating equal rights for people of color. Media outlets interrupted regular programming to provide coverage of these events taking place across the country. In New York City and St. Augustine, Florida, the atmosphere was charged with energy as thousands of everyday Americans demanded change. The University of Minnesota also participated in this movement, though its demonstrations were smaller and more intimate. Like many college students, Karen found herself glued to the television each day, watching the events unfold.

During finals week in early July, Karen visited the bus station to purchase a ticket to Lake City. When she returned to the Pi Beta Phi house, she found the girls huddled around the television, watching President Johnson address the nation before signing the Civil Rights Act. She took a moment to watch the historic event before calling Howard.

"We believe that all people are entitled to the blessings of liberty. However, millions are being denied these blessings—not due to their own failures, but because of the color of their skin."

Karen knew she could easily watch all night if she didn't pull away. A few minutes later, she dialed Howard's number on the house phone.

"Hello, Mrs. Boatman. I'm Karen. Has Howard told you I'm coming to Lake City over the Fourth of July holiday?"

"Who are you looking for?" the woman asked. "This is Mrs. Forthright."

"Oh," Karen replied, "I must have dialed the wrong number," and she hung up the receiver. She thought, *Surely he didn't give me the wrong number? Maybe I just misdialed it.*

She dialed again, and Mrs. Forthright picked up.

"Hello?"

"I'm looking for Howard Boatman. Is this the right phone number?" Karen asked.

"Which one?" Mrs. Forthright asked.

Now Karen was perplexed. "You mean there are two people named Howard Boatman?"

She heard another click as someone else picked up. "Who's the call for?" a woman asked.

Chapter 7

"Howard Boatman," Mrs. Forthright replied, "But we don't know if it's Junior or Senior. Any Boatmans on the line?"

There were more clicks as people got on the party line. They asked similar questions. *What is this?* she thought.

"A young lady is looking for Howard Boatman," Mrs. Forthright announced to the party line. "I'm assuming it's Junior. Is that correct, young lady?"

"This is Evelyn. Can I help you?" Howard's mother asked.

"Well… go ahead, young lady," Mrs. Forthright said.

"I am completely confused. I am looking for Howard Boatman," Karen repeated.

"Are you looking for my husband, or are you looking for my son?" Evelyn replied. "They are both named Howard."

"Howard Junior, I guess."

"He's not here. He's working out in the field right now. What can I do for you?"

"Well, my name is Karen. Mrs. Boatman, did he ever mention me? We go to the University of Minnesota together. He invited me to visit your farm over the Fourth of July holiday."

Karen overheard people saying, "Ohh."

"Ahh, yes," Evelyn recalled. "He mentioned that someone from the Cities was coming to visit. I'll let him know you called."

"Well, I bought my bus ticket, and I will arrive at the Lake City bus station around 2 tomorrow afternoon. Would you please ask him to pick me up?"

"He can't do that. He's going to be working in the fields at 2. You'll have to wait until he can pick you up in the evening. Why did you schedule a bus to come in the middle of the afternoon?"

"That's okay, Mrs. Boatman. I'll just get a cab to drop me off," Karen said. "Can you tell me your address, please?"

Karen heard snickering in the background.

"Karen, there are no taxis in Lake City," Evelyn responded. "Young lady, you'll just have to wait until he can come and pick you up. Goodbye."

Karen scoffed. Just before she hung up the receiver, she heard someone say, "Where are you from, dear? Chicago? New York?"

That was the weirdest telephone call in my life, she thought.

Chapter 7

To her surprise, Howard was waiting at the bus terminal.

"You made it!" Howard exclaimed as she entered the bus station. He offered to carry her suitcase as they headed toward his VW Beetle. "How was the trip?"

"It was long. I think we stopped in every small town along the way," Karen replied. She looked radiant in her periwinkle dress and shimmering pearls. Next to her, he shifted uneasily, his denim overalls and worn boots covered in the day's dirt and faint traces of grease.

"Thank you for meeting me, Howard. I believe it was your mother who mentioned that you wouldn't be able to pick me up until the evening."

"Yeah," Howard replied, rolling his eyes. "I told my parents that you're a special friend and that I needed to pick you up. My father wasn't happy about it."

"Should I have come at a different time?" Karen asked.

"No, it's fine," he replied. "Let me show you around town, then we'll drive back to the farm. I have to finish plowing the back 40 before dinner."

A few minutes later, with a cloud of dust trailing behind them, they pulled into the driveway at Howard's farm.

"Oh, so cute!" Karen replied. "This is your farm?" she looked at the white picket fence, the big red barn, and the perfectly manicured lawn.

"Yup, this is where I grew up."

"It's like a Norman Rockwell painting," she replied.

Howard grabbed her suitcase from the trunk, and they slipped through the side door, immediately greeted by the warm, woody aroma of the cedar-lined entryway. Ascending a short flight of stairs in the split-level home led them to another cedar-covered room, revealing a handmade wooden desk and a sewing nook presided over by an old Singer sewing machine, probably from the early 1900s.

"Mom!" Howard cried out. "Karen's here."

In the next room, Evelyn flattened dough in a spacious kitchen. Despite its generous size, it was dominated by antiquated cabinets and worn appliances. Howard approached his mother from behind, kissing the back of her head.

"Howard, my hands are full of dough," she scolded. "And you're full of dirt."

"Sorry, Mom," Howard grinned. He gestured for Karen to follow him. "Let me show you to the guestroom."

"Here we are," Howard proclaimed, setting down her suitcase. The room's cedar walls exuded that same

Chapter 7

warm, inviting fragrance from the entryway. In one corner, a single bed lay nestled amongst sewing supplies and a tidy pile of men's clothes. But Karen's eyes gravitated to the wooden desk, packed with an intriguing mix of souvenirs—each item a tangible memory of travels spanning the Middle East, Germany, China, Australia, and other distant lands. They smiled at each other and made their way back out to the kitchen.

Evelyn was still hard at work kneading dough. She stopped, glancing at Karen. "Well, don't just stand there. Introduce me."

"Mom, this is my friend from school, Karen."

"Nice to meet you, Mrs. Boatman," Karen replied.

"Do they teach you how to cook in Chicago?" Evelyn asked.

I'm not from Chicago, Karen mused. "Yes, my mom taught me how to cook," she replied smoothly.

"Good. You can help me by kneading this dough for the rolls tonight," Evelyn said.

"I need to finish plowing before supper," Howard said. "I'll leave you two ladies to prepare the meal. I should be done in about three hours."

Karen frowned, staring at Howard in alarm. *You're leaving me alone with her?* she thought, a flutter of anxiety stirring in her stomach. *This could be my future mother-in-law. I barely know her at all.* But Howard had already turned and set off towards the entryway, oblivious to her unease.

Karen turned back to Evelyn, who continued kneading the dough. She stood there for a moment, watching her work. "Is there a place I can go to wash up and change clothes? It's been a long trip from Minneapolis, and I'm in my nice dress."

Evelyn stopped, giving her a sharp look, then gestured to the kitchen sink. "Wash your hands right there, put on an apron, and help me mix this dough."

Karen frowned again. *But I'm so tired!* she thought. At the same time, she knew she had to make a good first impression. She dragged herself to the sink, washed her hands, donned an apron, and stood next to Evelyn.

"It needs another five minutes or so," Evelyn said as she walked away. Karen vaguely remembered how to knead dough, so she began pushing the dough down onto the cutting board. Meanwhile, Evelyn filled a pot with water and placed it on the stove to boil. She opened the refrigerator and took out a slab of meat, then looked back at Karen.

"No, no, you're doing that all wrong," she said. "You need to knead the dough like this…" Karen stepped aside as Evelyn began folding the dough, pressing it

Chapter 7

down with the heel of her hand and then turning it. "Keep doing this until the dough becomes elastic."

"Okay," she said, following her directions. It was much harder to do than it looked. A few minutes later, Evelyn checked her progress.

"You must knead faster. Put some muscle into it," Evelyn gave her a stern look before returning to the stove.

Karen sighed and started kneading faster. Eventually, the dough began to change texture.

"Well, I think I've done it," Karen proclaimed. Evelyn walked over and looked at Karen's handiwork.

"It's not great, but it will be okay. I'll work on this a little more. Can you stir the meat in the pot while I fix this dough?"

"Look," Karen said, her voice tight with fatigue. "I want to help you, but that was hard work. Just let me catch my breath for a second?"

"I need you to stir the pot on the stove. I can't do two things at once."

"Okay!" Karen snapped, "I'll stir the pot."

Evelyn tutted as Karen stirred the meat in the pot. She separated the dough into twelve pieces on a cookie sheet and walked back to the stove.

"I've been doing this alone for years, and I don't need your help," Evelyn said. "Why don't you adjust your attitude in the living room?"

"Fine," Karen said, walking into the next room and sitting down on the sofa. *Perhaps this was a mistake coming down here. She doesn't like me.* After taking a moment to freshen up in the bathroom, she returned to an orange armchair that welcomed her with a gentle embrace. *I'll just wait until Howard finishes in the field*, she decided, allowing herself to sink deeper into the cushions. The armchair was irresistibly comfortable, coaxing her into a drowsy relaxation.

A gentle nudge on her arm stirred her awake. As the evening sunlight streamed through the bay window, her gaze settled on a man standing beside her. His face was marked by the lines of time and toil, and his weathered skin told stories of a life spent outdoors. The denim overalls he wore were splattered with the grime of hard work, a testament to his days in the fields. "Hello," he said, his voice warm and inviting, accompanied by a smile that crinkled the corners of his eyes. "I'm Howard's father."

In that moment, a wave of relief washed over her. *Finally*, she thought, *someone nice to me!*

"I'm Karen," she replied, her voice steady as she introduced herself. "I attend the University of Minnesota with your son."

Chapter 7

"You're sitting in my chair," he replied, cocking his head at her.

"Oh, I'm sorry. I had no idea," Karen said, getting off the chair and sitting on the sofa.

He stared intently at her. "Howard should be back in a few minutes. The last time I checked, he had about an acre left to work on. He should finish just before sunset," he said before turning to leave and change into his clothes for supper.

Karen walked over to the bay window, admiring the vibrant summer landscape outside. *It really is beautiful here in the summer*, she thought to herself. *It's a shame that his parents are as cold as winter. I can see where Howard gets his emotionless demeanor from.*

Finally, just before the last bit of sunlight disappeared at 9 p.m., Howard walked in.

"Hi, Mom!" he sang, before sweeping into the living room to greet Karen. His arrival infused the house with a lively energy, a welcome cool breeze on a sweltering summer day.

"Are you ready for dinner?" he asked Karen.

"Sure," she replied, a beat of silence stretching slightly too long before her word escaped.

"I'll just be a minute while I get out of these clothes," he said and started to walk away. Looking back, he added, "I'm glad you're here."

Howard's dad strode into the kitchen and settled himself at the table. Evelyn joined him, her movements smooth and familiar. Karen paused, her gaze sweeping over the inviting kitchen scene before she approached the table and claimed a seat. The delicious sight and irresistible aroma of the golden-brown pot roast, tender carrots, sweet corn, fluffy rolls, and creamy mashed potatoes ignited a hunger that made her stomach grumble.

"Not there. That's Howard's seat," Evelyn scowled.

"Okay, sorry!" she mumbled, then hurried to the other place setting and slipped into the seat. No one spoke. The seconds felt like minutes as they waited in silence. Unsure of how to break the palpable tension, Karen selected a roll, nibbled a small piece, and set it on her plate.

"It's such a lovely night, don't you think?" she said with a bright smile, glancing at each of them. His dad was eyeing the roll she had just taken a bite of, while his mom looked at the clock.

"Howard, get in here this instant!" Evelyn bellowed. They heard Howard running down the hall.

"Sorry, Mom," he replied, smiling at Karen.

All three of them clasped their hands and said grace. Karen followed suit, pleased that the same dinner prayer was used at her family's house as well.

Chapter 7

"Did you finish up after your city distraction this afternoon?" his dad asked.

'City distraction?' Karen thought. *Was I a distraction?*

"Yes, I finished up," Howard said, taking a bite of pot roast.

"Good. Tomorrow I'm replacing the tires on the International before lunch. I'll need your help. In the afternoon, you can start cleaning out the silo."

"Harvest is not for another three months. The silo can wait. I've got a friend visiting me and I want to see her," he replied, glancing at Karen.

His dad looked at Karen in disgust. "Alright."

Throughout the meal, they sat in strained silence, the only sounds coming from the occasional clink of cutlery against porcelain plates. Karen could feel the weight of his parents' eyes upon her, scrutinizing her every move. Each fleeting glance felt like a judgment, an unspoken assessment. *I'm just trying to enjoy my meal!* she thought, frustration bubbling beneath her composed exterior.

"Can you show me around your farm?" she asked as they sat in the guestroom after dinner. "I'm excited to see it."

"Sure! That's a good idea."

As they walked into the warm embrace of the night, Karen couldn't help but smile. Millions of stars sparkled like little gems, dotting the beautiful canvas of the night sky. A chorus of crickets filled the air with their rhythmic symphony, harmonizing with the whispers of the night. The earthy scents of the farm mingled with the gentle, sweet fragrance of the grass, creating a delightful scent like nothing she had ever experienced. Tiny droplets of dew had formed on the grass blades, reflected in the light of the full moon above.

As they walked, Howard grabbed her hand and proceeded to show her the milk barn, chicken coop, and main barn. "At night, it's hard to see everything," he said. "Tomorrow afternoon, I'll take you around and show you the rest."

"What am I supposed to do in the morning while you're working?" she asked.

"Whatever you like, it's your vacation," he replied.

Karen hesitated, a question hovering on her lips. She took a deep breath. "What do your parents think of me?" she asked.

"I'm not sure," he said. "I haven't asked them about you since you arrived. Why?"

She chuckled softly. "No reason," she murmured, as a warmth creeped up her cheeks. "I'm just happy to be with you now."

He leaned in, and his lips, soft and warm, began a slow, tender exploration of hers. Karen's breath hitched, the lingering question about his parents dissolving like smoke as she melted into the embrace, lost in the delicate brush of his mouth.

"I'm glad you came."

It was the middle of the night when she woke up to the sound of pots and pans clanking in the kitchen. She heard both Howard and his father chatting in the hallway as she drifted back to sleep. A few hours later, she finally got up and looked out the guest room window. The midday sun cast sharp shadows from the oak tree just outside. There was no clock in the room, and she didn't have a watch. She could hear a knife striking a cutting board, along with the enticing scents of baked beans and fried chicken. *I better get moving*, she thought. She took a shower and got dressed, ready for an afternoon of fun on the farm. Soon after, she heard Howard and his dad walk in together for lunch.

Chapter 7

There was a knock on her door. "Karen!" Howard asked. "Would you like some lunch?"

"I'll be right there," she called out, finessing the blend of her eye shadow. She wore a lightweight sheath dress and flats. Looking back at the mirror, she smiled and thought, *Today is going to be a better day. After all, it's the Fourth of July! Nobody works on the Fourth of July.*

She bounded into the kitchen. "Good morning, everyone!" Three heads, already seated at the table, looked up at her, their expressions a blend of weary patience and irritation. Howard's dad, his overalls covered in dirt and grime, glanced at the clock as Karen took her seat. Meanwhile, Evelyn studied Karen's dress with interest as they prayed.

"How did you sleep?" Evelyn inquired, handing her a hotdish.

"Good," Karen mumbled.

"How late did you two stay up?" she continued, looking at Howard.

"Not very late, Mom. I just showed her around the farm."

"So, then why did you sleep all morning?" Evelyn asked Karen.

Karen weighed her words. "Well, I woke up in the middle of the night to the sound of pots and pans banging in the kitchen. The next thing I knew, it was almost noon. I guess I slept through the entire morning."

"Hmph," Evelyn replied, taking a bite of hotdish.

Karen shook her head, feeling her good mood slip away.

Later that afternoon, Howard was attempting to teach Karen how to operate the Ford tractor.

"Just like a car, you have the clutch over here," he pointed to the pedal near her left foot, "and the brake pedals over here," he pointed to her right foot. "The accelerator is this lever, and the transmission has five speeds and reverse."

"Back in high school, my friends and I would drive to the bars in Wisconsin," she said. "But it was an automatic transmission. Can you show me how to do this?"

"Sure, of course," he said, his gaze following Karen as she slid from the tractor. With a fluid movement, he took her place, then glanced at her, tapping his thigh. A playful sparkle in her eye, she swung back up, fitting neatly beside him. A soft giggle escaped her as she steadied herself, her arm finding its familiar place around his back. He turned, his smile warm and genuine, and their lips met in a sweet, simple kiss just as Howard let out the clutch.

Chapter 7

"Whoop!" Karen screamed as they puttered around the farm at 2 miles an hour.

After a delightful afternoon together, it was time for supper.

"Can we go to a restaurant tonight instead of eating with your parents?" Karen asked. It sounded like the perfect way to end a wonderful afternoon. "We could go to that A&W drive-in you told me about."

"No! Not there!" Howard replied, shaking his head. "How about a nice sit-down restaurant instead?"

"Sure, whatever you think," she replied.

The Iron Horse in Lake City pulsed with the energy of the holiday crowd, a vibrant tapestry of chattering tourists and clattering silverware. The mouth-watering aroma of sizzling steaks lured diners from every corner of the restaurant. As they settled into their booth, her smile, already fragile, finally crumbled. "I don't think your parents care for me," she admitted, the words barely audible against the bustling crowd.

Howard took a sip of his water. "Yeah, they gave me an earful at breakfast this morning."

"What did they say?"

Howard hesitated for a moment before blurting it out. "My mom thinks you're lazy and have no concept of hard work."

"That's not true! I helped her knead bread before she kicked me out of her kitchen for not doing it right. Besides, I'm a guest in her home!"

"Is it true that you sat in my dad's chair in the living room?"

"Yes, but I had no idea I wasn't allowed to sit there," Karen protested.

Howard sighed. "I see. That's my dad's chair, and when he saw you sleeping in it, he got a little upset."

"How was I supposed to know that?" she asked. "I apologized to him. Did he mention that?"

"He needs my help on the farm, and he thinks you are distracting me from my duties."

Karen's jaw tightened. "Fine. If I'm such a distraction, then maybe I should *go*." The words were sharper than intended; her voice was tense with suppressed frustration. "I tried my best to be nothing but pleasant and respectful to them. But I'm sorry, Howard, your parents are just—cold."

"I'll talk to them."

"And tell them what, exactly? 'Don't be so cold?' A zebra can't change its stripes," she hissed. "Face it, they

Chapter 7

don't like me, and I don't like them. I'll catch a bus back to Minneapolis tonight."

"No, please don't do that."

"Howard, I'm not going back there."

"But what about the Fourth of July fireworks tonight? I was going to introduce you to my best friend, Dick!"

Karen leveled a stare at him.

"Okay, okay! We'll head back to the farm after supper and grab your things."

"No, I want to leave now. *You* will head back to the farm, and I will meet you at the bus station!" she said. "I'm not going back there ever again."

"Can we at least enjoy a nice meal together?" Howard pleaded.

Karen got out of the booth and put her hands on her hips.

Howard closed his eyes and let out a deep sigh. They walked out of the restaurant without even telling the waitress to cancel their meals.

"Really, so you left on the Fourth?" Ellie asked.

"Yes, I caught the last bus out of town. I watched the Minneapolis fireworks from the seat of a Greyhound bus as we pulled into town," Karen said, taking a drag from her cigarette. "I couldn't take it anymore, Ellie. I felt extremely uncomfortable there."

"Didn't I tell you? You're just not a farmer's wife," Patty said.

Karen rolled her eyes and looked at the wall. "Yes, you did."

"I have an idea," Ellie said with a mischievous grin as she walked over to her closet and pulled out a bottle of vodka.

"You smuggled that in here?" Karen whispered. "God, we could get in huge trouble."

She reached into the dorm fridge and took out three cans of Coca-Cola.

"As long as we keep it down, no one will know," Ellie said. "Besides, you could use a drink."

As summer came to a close, she knew it was time to end her relationship with Howard. But how would she do it?

While leaving Coffman Union after a day of studying, she noticed many students gathered to watch the Democratic National Convention.

"What's all the fuss about?" Karen asked a student.

Chapter 7

"President Johnson is about to announce his running mate. There are two former Gophers, Eugene McCarthy and Hubert Humphrey, who are strong contenders."

She decided to eat supper at Coffman Union while watching the convention. President Johnson teased the audience, withholding the name of his choice for vice president. He highlighted the candidate's qualities and emphasized the strengths of the ticket in his deep Texas drawl. Finally, he shared his secret with the delegates.

"I hope you will choose, as the next vice president of the United States, my close friend and longtime colleague, Senator Hubert Humphrey of Minnesota."

She walked back to the Pi Beta Phi house. Taped to her door was a phone message from Howard. He'd called during supper and said he would call back the next day at the same time.

She weighed her options. *The Pi Phis are coming back next week, and I have to move to Comstock Hall. I could say I'm busy and avoid his call*, she thought. *No, that won't work. I need to confront him.* She resolved to be in the house for his call.

"How is summer school going?" Howard asked in a playful tone. "Are you enjoying Greek life?"

"There are a few Greeks here, but most of us are not sisters," Karen replied. "I'm thinking about going to the rush week event for Pi Beta Phi. I like the house. There's a lot of camaraderie here."

"I can give you some tips on how to stand out during recruitment events," Howard said.

"Sure," Karen replied cooly. They fell silent for a moment.

"I'm excited to be back on campus next week!" he continued with his cheerful tone. "How about we kick off the new quarter with a picnic together on The Lawn before classes start?"

"That sounds lovely, Howard, and I appreciate the invitation. But I have a lot going on right now. I'm moving into Comstock Hall, and I have my finals coming up. Could we meet at Coffman Union for coffee instead?"

"Sure," Howard replied, sounding deflated.

"What day are you back on campus?" she asked.

"I'm leaving on Saturday morning from Lake City."

"Good. I'll see you Coffman Union on Sunday at noon?"

"Sure," Howard muttered, his cheerful tone vanished.

Chapter 7

After church on Sunday, she strode to Coffman Union, continuing to refine her speech as she went.

I've really enjoyed our dates. We shared some wonderful moments. However, we come from different backgrounds; I was raised in a bustling city, while you spent your childhood on a farm. Our aspirations for life after college don't align. Howard, this wasn't meant to be.... Perfect! Short and sweet, five minutes at most.

Everything was going according to plan; she would be there 15 minutes early.

She bought a coffee, added cream and sugar, and searched for a semi-private spot.

Howard's shout of "Karen!" echoed across Coffman Union as he sprang from his seat, his arm flailing in an enthusiastic welcome. He'd beaten her to the meeting, looking sharp and polished in his formal attire—a world away from the grimy denim he wore while toiling on the farm during the Fourth.

"It's so good to see you!" he said as she approached. "Please join me."

She sat down and started her speech. "Howard, we had some good times together—"

"Yes, we did. Every time we're together, we have a wonderful time. Watching *Dr. Zhivago*, playing roulette at the Student Union, and our date at Vescio's were all memorable. Even showing you how to run the Ford tractor was fun. I've had a lot of time to think about us while we were apart, and I'm looking forward to spending more time with you this fall!"

"I agree we had some wonderful moments, but—"

"Yes, I know what you're going to say—you dislike my parents," he said, looking down at the table. "They made assumptions about you just because you're from the big city. They regret it now."

"That's our problem, Howard! I grew up in a large city outside Chicago, while you grew up on a rural farm. We come from different worlds," she said, shaking her head.

"Relationships are so much more than just finding someone who shares your personality or interests. If that were the case, things could get pretty boring fast! The magic happens when you connect with someone who encourages you to grow and explore new ideas. Even if you have different values or beliefs, those differences can spark meaningful conversations and exciting experiences. Sharing different viewpoints not only broadens your understanding of the world but also helps you grow as a person. In the end, these dynamics make your relationship richer and allow both of you to learn and thrive together."

Karen's brows lifted in outright disbelief. This profound statement was utterly unexpected from Howard, whose relationship capacity had always seemed, at best, juvenile.

Howard continued. "Building a successful relationship is akin to baking a blueberry pie. It demands an abundance of respect, a rich dialogue filled with open communication, unwavering trust, and a dash of patience—plus a cup or two of faith to bind it all together. If even one of these vital ingredients is missing, the pie will lack its delicious flavor and delightful taste."

Leave it to Howard to relate love to food, she thought.

"It occurs to me," Karen mused, "that we're both only children. That often cultivates a drive for perfection and a focus on achievement, but it can also manifest as selfishness and a tendency toward being pampered. Because of this, both of us prefer to control the situation."

"Absolutely!" he replied. "Do you remember our night at the Iron Horse? I drove back to the farm, packed your things, and met you at the bus station. I thought you were a little selfish to leave, but you had your mind made up. What I remember most vividly, though, was watching your bus pull away. It felt like someone was tearing something I loved away from me. I felt powerless."

Karen's heart softened.

"Do you remember the cattle ranch proposal I mentioned?"

"Yes, of course. You're very excited about it."

"I talked to my dad about it a month ago. After he read it, he kept asking, 'We have a good thing going here. Why would you want to change the formula?' He also criticized the idea of directly marketing to customers, insisting that I'm not a salesperson."

"That's terrible," she said. "So, what are you gonna do?"

"Once I own the farm, he won't be able to stop me. I still believe it will succeed; I just need to approach the situation differently with him," he said, meeting her gaze. "I share this with you because, as an only child, you understand why I have faith that it will work."

He was correct, of course. Howard, fueled by a singular purpose, refused to be deterred, just as Karen had embraced her passion for the viola and her fervent dedication to attend a distant college far from Rockford.

"Look Karen, I truly believe we can support each other as we work through the frustrations we feel about our childhoods. Let's lean on one another—we can find a way to get through it together."

Karen was not expecting this outpouring of feelings from him. No man had ever told her this before.

Howard continued. "You have encouraged me to say how I feel. Well, when I'm with you, it's like my life resets again. I'm calm and clear-headed. I feel like I can just be myself. Remember what you told me during our first date in the Bailey Hall lobby?"

"No."

"Right after I gave you the flowers, as we were heading out the door to meet Paul and Diane in the Model A, you said, 'Let's create some memories.'"

"I did?" Karen said.

Howard chuckled. "I remember last spring. I was having a terrible day. I was creating the final report for my internship, and my typewriter broke. I dreaded pulling an all-nighter after work. But you came by the Dining Center and gave me a cherry pie and smiled so sweetly at me. And life wasn't so bad," Howard said. "You see, Karen, it's the things you say and do that make it special to be around you."

She looked around the dining room, struggling for the right words. Nothing was coming to her.

"Are you dating someone else?" he finally asked. "I've heard there was a baseball player you—"

Chapter 7

"No, no!" she said, looking at him. "I was not expecting this."

"What were you expecting?" he asked.

"It's not important."

"That offer to go on a picnic is still open," he smiled.

Karen pursed her lips together. "Okay, I will go on a picnic with you. But there are a few conditions if I go on another date with you. First, I do not want to live my life on a farm. I did not attend school for four years to cook, clean, and care for children all day. I am not a farmer's wife," she said. "If this relationship goes any further, you have to agree that we will not live on a farm."

Howard frowned, his lips pressed tightly in a mask of contemplation as he studied the worn, weathered surface of the table, its grain worn smooth from years of use. An uncomfortable silence wrapped around him like a heavy blanket, thick and unyielding. Karen watched him closely, a knot of anxiety twisting in her stomach; she feared he might rise abruptly and walk away. Farming was the only world he truly understood, and she was asking him to give it up for her.

"I'll think about it," he replied.

A wave of shock washed over Karen, and her suspicious gaze locked onto his eyes. *Surely not*, she thought. His eyes glistened, not with hope, but with a sheen of unshed tears and a crushing resignation. They conveyed a silent plea: *What more can I do to make you understand?*

Karen continued. "You need to become more emotionally open with me. This is the first time you've expressed your emotions to me. I need to see more of that, or we have no future together."

"Okay."

Karen closed her eyes. "Tell me what color eyes I have."

"Brown."

She opened her eyes and smiled at him, "Finally, I agree that we have a shared childhood trauma of being only children. But is that the *only* thing we have in common?"

Howard thought for a moment. "We both manage our responsibilities well. We are independent and dislike being told what to do. However, we can be self-centered and sometimes struggle with emotional issues."

"Well, I'm impressed," Karen said. "When do you want to go on our picnic?"

"How about right now?" he replied, a big grin on his face.

Karen laughed. "Well, we're going to need a picnic basket and some food. We can't have wine since we're

Chapter 7

on campus, but we should bring water or something to drink."

"I have everything ready to go. The house mother stored the sandwiches, fruit, and sodas in the refrigerator, and I have chips and chocolate in the picnic basket that's sitting in my room at the fraternity."

Karen cocked her head and smiled. "So, what if I told you I wanted to break up with you today?" she said.

Howard smiled. "I knew you wouldn't."

Chapter 8

An outraged chorus of students in the SPSC's television room shouted in disbelief at the screen, "He's running the wrong way!" a voice exclaimed, followed by exasperated murmurs. "Of all the idiotic things."

"I still don't understand what happened," Karen asked Howard. "I mean, he picked up the football, and he scored a touchdown."

"Yes, but Marshall went to the wrong end zone. That was the Vikings' end zone."

"OK, so they got the touchdown, not the Vikings?"

"Well, they got points but not a touchdown. When a team is caught in their end zone, the other team is awarded a safety, which is worth only two points. They also get the ball back."

"Howard, this game is so confusing."

After the game, they went out to a drive-in in Dinkytown.

"The Vikings were fortunate today. If they had lost the game because of that safety, I don't think Jim Marshall could ever live that down." Howard said.

Karen had been distracted since the game; her usual outgoing demeanor had given way to thoughtful quietness. "Is everything all right, Karen?" he asked gently. "You haven't said much since the game ended."

She took a deep breath. "I've been thinking a lot about us lately. Things feel solid. Especially after your parents apologized to us about the Fourth of July weekend."

"Yeah, I agree."

"Well, it makes me want to take another step. Would you consider coming to Rockford with me for Christmas to meet my family?"

"Sure! That's a great idea!" Howard replied.

"Great! I'll talk to my family about it during my call on Sunday."

"And I'll talk to my family about it over Thanksgiving. When we go to Illinois, we can take my car."

"Yes, the interstate system through Wisconsin was nearly complete during my last trip to Illinois. It makes

Chapter 8

the journey much faster; it now takes only six hours to drive from Minneapolis to Rockford."

"I've never been to Illinois. How far away do you live from Chicago?"

"Rockford is about an hour west of Chicago. It's almost a suburb."

"Well," Dick said from the underside of his VW Beetle, trying to loosen the oil plug. "If I were in your shoes, I would wait until Friday or Saturday night. Your mom's not gonna like this at all."

"Good idea," Howard replied as he opened the rear engine compartment and loosened the oil cap. "I could bring it up Friday night. Your parents invited us over for dinner on Saturday night."

As the old engine oil streamed out of the car, Dick rolled out from underneath the Beetle and looked at Howard. "Oh, they did?" He grabbed a new oil filter.

"Since we are both home for the holidays, our moms thought it was a good idea. When you guys owned the farm, we used to get together Saturday nights for dinner once a month. I looked forward to that."

"Yeah, me too," Dick added.

Dick screwed on the new oil filter and replaced the oil plug. "Okay, all set," he announced as he rolled away from the undercarriage. "So, what are you going to say?"

"So, I'll be spending Christmas with Karen's family," he said, the words a bit monotone as he carefully poured new oil into the Beetle's small crankcase hole. "I'm going to tell them she invited me, and that things are getting pretty serious between us. It feels like the right thing to do, you know—the next step. I'll swing by after we drive home, and we can do our Christmas then."

His mom stared at him, her fork clattering onto her plate. "You're what!?" she finally exploded, her voice thick with disbelief. He froze, the taste of blueberry pie suddenly lodged in his throat.

"Mom, she came here over the summer. Now it's my turn to go down and see her parents."

"Not over Christmas, son," his dad replied. "That's family time."

Howard pursed his lips and exhaled through his nose. "Our relationship has gotten more serious. She invited me down, and I want to go."

Chapter 8

"Howard, listen," his mother began. "I know you. Better than anyone in this world. In my view, Karen is not the right person for you. She has certain... expectations of men, and you will find it difficult to meet her emotional and financial needs over time. Is that something you want?"

"What your mother is trying to say," his father continued, "is that she won't be truly happy here on the farm. Karen is a beautiful woman, Howard, but this life—it isn't for everyone. She's not built for the daily grind of running a farm. She's a city girl, through and through. She will crave new things, the latest trends. In the long run, son, it just won't work."

"I see," Howard replied, a weary look crossing his face as he met his mother's pained expression. "I promise, once we're back from Illinois, I'll head straight back here the following day. We can celebrate Christmas then."

Howard watched a tear roll down his mother's face. "After all we've done for you, Howard. This woman isn't forever, and you're going to skip Christmas at home to be with her? Years from now, you will look back on this decision and regret it."

"She's right, son," his dad replied. "We have done a lot for you. We've paid for your school, and we're giving you this farm. This would be the first Christmas that you haven't spent here. Your mother and I would be heartbroken. This isn't something we are willing to compromise on. Period. End of discussion." His father's voice cut off any further protest, the words hanging heavy in the air.

Howard rose from the table, making a slow, despondent circuit around the kitchen. *First, the cattle farm, a dream his father had dismissed as ridiculous. Now, Karen.*

His stare locked onto his father. "I'm going," he asserted, every syllable cutting through the silence. He walked to the living room, drawn to the impenetrable darkness of the night through the bay window. From the kitchen, his mother's weeping cut through the tense silence. Howard's jaw tightened as he noticed the subtle trembling of his hands.

Howard turned up the AM radio as the weather forecast came over the VW Beetle's speakers.

"Snow is expected overnight in southern Wisconsin, with accumulations of 2 to 6 inches. The heaviest snowfall will occur in the early evening and taper off by morning, potentially reaching an inch per hour."

"Where are we now?" Howard asked Karen as the snow started to get thicker and accumulate on the interstate.

"We're about two hours away," Karen said with regret in her voice. "We should've left sooner."

"Well, no sense crying about that now."

"Howard, I don't know if we can make it." Karen's voice rose, edged with panic. "Maybe we shouldn't push it. We should find a hotel."

I'm not stopping, he thought to himself. *I need to find a way to distract her.*

"Hey, I'd love to hear more about your childhood!" Howard said with a smile. "What's a fun story or memory that your parents like to share about you when you were growing up?"

"Hmm," Karen thought for a moment. "When I was little, my mom taught me how to make pistachio pudding. I love it, especially with big pistachios."

"Wow! You never told me that before?" Howard exclaimed, his head briefly turning to Karen before it darted back to the swirling blizzard.

"Well, that's when times were good. Before they told me..." Karen stopped cold.

"Told you what?"

Karen let out a deep sigh. "I guess you're gonna find out sometime, better to hear it from me now. Howard, I was adopted."

"Really?" His head snapped toward her, his brow furrowing in confusion. She sat there, her chin tucked,

Chapter 8

and her gaze locked onto her lap as if it held the weight of the world. *This makes sense*, he thought, a complex swirl of concern and curiosity churning within him. He glanced once more at the oncoming flurry of snowflakes.

"Why didn't you tell me this before? This is important," he said, looking back at her.

"I was afraid you would break up with me," she said, starting to sob. "I'm sorry. I'm a terrible person for not telling you."

Howard grappled with the decision of whether to pull over to and comfort Karen or to persist in their slow crawl toward Rockford. The car crept along at a sluggish 20 miles per hour, the world outside a blur of white against a darkening background. He collected his thoughts, weighing the urgency of their journey against the need to support her in this difficult moment.

"You're not a terrible person. I'm just curious why you didn't tell me this before?" he looked at Karen, still gazing at her lap. "Are you… ashamed… of being adopted?"

"They told me one evening after piano practice that they weren't my biological parents. I wanted to meet my real parents, but they wouldn't let me."

Howard caught a glimpse of Karen's face, instantly catching the angry eyes and the tight set of her jaw before he returned his attention to the treacherous road.

"I didn't believe them, so I walked to the adoption center the next morning before school. The social worker told me it was a closed adoption."

"What's a closed adoption?" Howard asked.

"When both sets of parents agree to have no contact on the adoption form. It means they leave no address, no phone number, nothing."

"So, you have no idea who your real parents are?"

"Nope, and I never will, thanks to them."

"That's awful," Howard said. "How old were you? You said you walked to the adoption center?"

"Thirteen."

"Why did they wait so long to tell you?" he asked, looking back at her.

"I don't know," Karen stated, her voice tight with suppressed emotion as she faced Howard. "That day shattered everything between us. I remember being so carefree and completely whole until then. But they can't undo what they did, and the trust we shared simply evaporated. When I graduated from Rockford West, I dreamt of moving to New York. but moving so far away troubled my family," she said, shaking her head. "After endless discussions, we finally compromised—instead of attending Columbia in New

Chapter 8

York with Georgene, I would choose a school in the Midwest. I picked Concordia, a Lutheran college in Minnesota."

An ominous silence clung to the car, broke only by the swish of the wiper blades.

Karen took a Kleenex out of her purse and cleaned up her mascara in the visor's mirror.

"Howard, you have shown me such devotion. I can't explain the feeling of peace I feel when I'm with you," she said, her voice still shaking. "I knew you would understand."

"Of course I understand."

As they stared at the oncoming snowflakes getting larger, they sat in silence, gazing out at the road. They passed a distance sign that read, 'Rockford 25 miles.'

"Just a little further now," Karen said. Howard looked at the speedometer: 15 miles an hour.

Then, without warning, a monstrous gust of wind shoved the car violently sideways. A terrifying shriek of ice erupted beneath the tires, dragging them closer towards the unseen, snow-choked shoulder. Howard white-knuckled the steering wheel, feeling his Beetle slide and buck, as he forced it back towards the barely visible road. *That was close*, he thought. *I need to keep distracting her.* He glanced over at Karen; her eyes were wide with fear.

"I've spent some time reflecting on what you said about living on the farm. I can appreciate why you feel that life is not for you. However, farming is the only life I have known besides college. I'm at a crossroads; and it's time to choose." Howard paused. He could feel Karen's stare as he gripped the Beetle's steering wheel tightly. "Therefore, I've decided to look for a job in Agri banking."

"Seriously?" Karen said, "You're giving up your dream for a cattle farm? What did your parents say?"

Howard looked over at her for a split second. "Karen, I said I'm thinking about it. I have not decided yet. And I haven't told my parents I'm looking for a banking position, either. Graduation is just five months away, making this the ideal time to launch a job search. Interviews are windows to your future—they require no commitment but open doors to possibilities."

Howard felt a current of warmth flow from Karen's gaze and instinctively turned to meet her eyes. For a precious, fleeting second, the world outside faded into insignificance. A genuine smile spread across his face.

"Keep your eyes on the road, mister."

Chapter 9

Karen shook off the last clinging snowflakes from her coat and hair, embracing the glorious rush of indoor warmth. Howard set down the suitcases and eased the front door shut, sealing out Old Man Winter. A wave of intoxicating fresh pine filled the room, emanating from a magnificent, eight-foot Douglas fir that commanded the living room. It was decorated with a lifetime of cherished ornaments, a sparkling cascade of twinkling lights, and shimmering silver garlands – perhaps a touch too grand for the space, yet perfectly charming. Beneath its branches, an assortment of presents—both big and small—waited eagerly for their lucky recipients. *They're really going all out to make this a special Christmas!* Karen thought with a smile. *We've never had a real Christmas tree before. We always used the Evergleam from the Sears catalog.*

"We've been so worried!" Olga exclaimed as she hugged her daughter. "Your father and I have been watching out the window for your car for hours."

.

"We should have left earlier in the morning," Karen admitted.

"The weather turned nasty after we started heading south from Madison," Howard explained to Porter. "Howard Boatman," he added, removing his gloves and extending his hand.

"Nice to meet you. I'm Porter Smith, and this is my wife, Olga."

"Karen told us you're a farmer. What do you grow?" Porter asked, taking a sip of hot chocolate.

"We alternate between corn and soybeans on 85 acres. We also raise pigs, cows, and chickens. It's a second-generation farm."

"I've never been on a farm before!" Olga exclaimed. "Karen mentioned a few things about it. What's it like?"

"You're always busy on the farm," Howard said, his eyes drifting into the past. "You know, ever since I was little, I would wake up early to help out with the chores. It feels like you're always out in the field, taking care of the animals, cleaning up the barn, or fixing things. There's so much to do.

"My mom would take a trip to town once a month to stock up on groceries. Sometimes, I'd grab a few things

Chapter 9

we needed after school, but for the most part, we were self-sufficient. Still are. We grow vegetables and butcher our own meat."

"What about winter? I've heard it lasts for months, and it's very snowy. Do you buy food at the grocery store when you can't grow anything?"

"My mom and I do a ton of canning over the summer. We preserve a variety of vegetables, including tomatoes, peas, corn, and pickles, as well as fruits such as strawberries, blueberries, and apples. By the time harvest rolls around, we have two full shelves of canned goods in the basement to get us through the winter.

"During heavy snowstorms like this one, travel is limited to sleds. We can only drive into town once Big Red clears the roads, which sometimes takes days."

"What's Big Red?" Porter asked.

"Oh! That's the name of the road grader that maintains our dirt roads. After a snowstorm, everything is still and quiet, so everyone knows when Big Red is coming up Sugerloaf Pass. People stop what they are doing and come out to wave. Usually, the mailman's Jeep follows along, bringing some mail, too."

Karen had never heard of canning before. "So, you put fruits and vegetables in a jar, and they stay good all winter long? That doesn't make much sense. Won't they go bad after a week?"

"Canning is a food preservation method that uses a Mason jar and a specialized, self-sealing lid. First, you boil the food, then carefully transfer it into sterilized glass jars. The lid and screw band are then applied. Next, the filled jars are boiled in a water bath until they are vacuum-sealed."

Porter asked. "And you process your own meat?"

"Yes, we do. My grandfather taught me how to butcher and cure meat. During the warmer months, we slaughter cows and pigs. Then every fall, after the harvest, we obtain our hunting permits in town and go deer hunting. If we're lucky, we get two deer each year."

"You'll stay here tonight," Porter said to Howard, opening the door to the guest room. The cozy space featured a single bed neatly made with a deep blue comforter and a bedside table adorned with a small lamp. The walls were decorated with an eclectic collection of photographs that captured precious moments: Olga and Porter's wedding day, trips to Chicago, and an array of pictures showcasing Karen at various ages, from her first steps to graduation.

Chapter 9

"Sleep well," Porter said with a friendly smile before gently closing the door. Howard took a moment to absorb his surroundings, his eyes drifting from one photograph to the next, each telling a story filled with love. After a couple of minutes, he heard a quiet, tentative knock at the door as Karen entered.

"Hey! How are you?" she asked, leaning against the doorframe. Her eyes sparkled with pride and nostalgia as she looked around the room. "There are lots of pictures of me growing up in here."

"I noticed that!" he replied with a cheeky grin. He stepped closer, lightly touched her face, and leaned in for a sweet kiss. "But why don't we share your room? Your big bed looks super comfy," he said, pointing to his single bed. "And I'm stuck with this tiny bed that's way too small for me!" He made a sad face, and she couldn't help but laugh.

"I told you... My parents are pretty traditional," she whispered back with a smile. "Since we aren't married, you have to have your own room."

The next morning, Howard and Porter began shoveling the driveway while Karen and Olga prepared breakfast.

"So, how did you meet him?" Olga asked, stirring the pancake mix.

"He's an Aggie, and we met at his fraternity one Saturday night."

"What's an Aggie?" Olga asked.

Karen cracked an egg into a mixing bowl. "It's a fraternity. Alpha Gamma Rho. Its members are known as Aggies because it's an agricultural fraternity."

"Karen, he's undeniably kind and respectful, embodying that honest, hardworking farm ethic. But beneath it all, there's a definite emotional distance, isn't there?"

Karen sighed. "There is. He gets that from his parents. I've asked him to express his feelings more, but it's difficult for him to do that. However, when I open up to him, he is a great listener and very supportive. We had a constructive conversation on the way down."

"What did you talk about?" she asked.

Karen's lips pressed into a thin line as she whisked the eggs, the golden yolks churning into a frothy swirl in the bowl. "I told him I was adopted," she finally confessed, her voice filled with apprehension. The unspoken words hung heavy between them.

Olga expertly poured the thick pancake batter onto the sizzling cast-iron skillet, watching as one, two, and then three small round pancakes bubbled softly, their edges crisping perfectly. The warm, inviting aroma

Chapter 9

began to fill the air, mingling with the scent of fresh coffee.

Finally, Olga broke the silence. "We didn't mean to hurt you."

"Mom," Karen replied without hesitation. "Please don't make a scene about this in front of Howard. I really like him, and I want this to work out."

"We made a mistake. We shouldn't have waited —"

"I don't want to talk about it anymore. Please stop."

"This high school is huge!" he said. "So, is there a Rockford East too?"

Karen chuckled. "Yes. And there's a third one too, Rockford Central. That's the original high school. It's even bigger than Rockford East and West."

They drove by Guzzardo's Music and stopped for a milkshake at The Last Straw.

"If we're lucky," Karen said. "Someone will be having a birthday, and they'll bring out the Fire Engine Special."

"What's that?"

"It's a special malt they serve for people's birthdays. Red lights and sirens go off, and all the employees get involved. It's fun to watch."

As night fell, they drove downtown to see the new neon lighting project and the holiday displays in the shop windows.

"My grandfather told me that Miss Wisconsin and Miss Illinois were here to flip the switch on the neon lights a few months ago. There are lots of new shops now."

Howard was impressed with the Christmas displays in the windows. "The Red Owl and most restaurants decorate for Christmas in Lake City, but nothing like this."

As they wandered around the downtown area, Karen asked, "How are you getting along with my dad?" Karen asked.

"Pretty good! I like him. We had a good chance to talk this morning while shoveling snow."

"What did you talk about?"

"He talked about his job as a machinist at Barber-Colman. He's been there for quite a while. He remembered how close the three of you were back in elementary school. Everyone was so proud when you became a Sunday school teacher at his father-in-law's church! Things changed in middle and high school after the whole adoption mess, but he really respects his father-in-law, Pastor Swenson, who kept everything together during those times. Now that you're living far away, he misses you a lot."

Chapter 9

On the way home, they drove by her grandparents' house. Karen said, "I wish we had more time! I'd love to introduce you to my grandparents right now, but we really need to get back for supper. My mom is making something special for us."

"Well, can't we just go in and say hello? It only takes five minutes," Howard asked.

"I guess you're right. We do have time for that," Karen said as Howard pulled into the driveway.

"This was a great idea," Karen said as they approached the weathered front steps. For a second, she was back, not just remembering, but feeling the ghost of her younger self on the snow-covered lawn. The shouts of her friends, thin and bright, pierced the air as they played Red Light, Green Light. The house, blessedly, stood exactly as she remembered. The front door swung open, and Grandpa, his eyes crinkling with genuine delight, pulled her into a hug. His familiar, solid embrace was a balm to her soul. "I'm so glad you came by," he rumbled.

"I missed you so much, Grandpa!" Karen burst out, her heart swelling with warmth. She introduced Howard, her friend from college, and after a few brief minutes, they headed back to the Beetle. "See you tomorrow!" she called, her excitement palpable as they walked back to the car, glancing back at the welcoming house that held so many cherished memories.

As they had done in previous years, they attended Good Shepherd on Christmas Eve and then went to Trinity for her grandfather's Christmas sermon. But this year, with their Douglas fir, Olga and Porter would host Christmas dinner.

Karen woke up early on Christmas morning to help her mother with dinner.

"Have you spoken with Pam?" her mother asked, peeling the potatoes.

"No."

"You should call her and try to get together before you leave!" her mom said. "Her mother told me she was coming home from college for Christmas, so I know she's home."

"If there's time, I'll call her," she said as she continued to set the table.

"I like Howard," her mother said. "When I sat next to him at Good Shepherd, I could tell he believed in God. Is he Lutheran?"

"Yes, Mom. Lutheran, Missouri Synod."

Chapter 9

"I could tell. He knew the Apostles' Creed by heart. When you left Concordia, I thought you had given up on trying to find a nice Lutheran boy."

"Okay, Mom,"

"Did you hear on the news about the car bomb that almost killed Bob Hope in Vietnam?" Porter asked as he sliced the ham. Most of the table shook their heads.

"That's awful. I'll pray for his family tonight," Grandpa said.

At Christmas dinner, Howard became the center of attention. Both Dad and Grandpa were interested in his rural upbringing on a farm.

"Do you play any musical instruments, Howard?" Olga asked.

"No, there was no time for learning an instrument on the farm," Howard replied.

"Karen plays two instruments: the piano and viola," she said to Howard. "I taught her how to play piano. She used to play it for her Sunday school class every week."

"I see," Howard said, taking a bite of mashed potatoes.

"Then, one day, she didn't want to play anymore. She broke my heart. Howard, do you know why she didn't want to play anymore?"

"Mom," Karen said, shaking her head. "Don't do this."

"Olga, please," her grandfather added. "We are having a nice meal here."

"No, I need this, and I may never get another chance," she said, measuring her words as she locked her gaze on Howard. "She stopped playing after we told her she was adopted. And she has blamed me for it ever since." She glared at Karen. "Last Christmas, you walked out of this house, unfairly blaming your father and me for hiding your biological parents from you. I cried for weeks afterwards. Weeks!" she whispered, letting that sink in. "You were 13 when we told you about the adoption, and I know you saw the social worker the very next day. You know this was a closed adoption. Now that you are a grown woman, I have to ask: why do you still blame us? It was your biological parents who chose a closed adoption, not your father and me. We had no choice. It's time for you to confront the truth instead of directing your anger at me."

Suddenly, Karen was back at Easter dinner, the one from her senior year, feeling the weight of her mother's disappointment over her decision to attend Concordia College in Minnesota. *I knew this was going to happen*, she thought to herself.

Karen closed her eyes. "May I be excused?" she asked, her voice barely a whisper. Her grandfather nodded slowly, his gaze following her as she rose and moved down the hallway, disappearing into the quiet sanctuary of her bedroom. Grandpa looked at Olga, a shadow crossing his face before he pushed back his chair. His footsteps were light as he approached her door. He rapped softly, the gentle sound echoing through the house's stillness.

"Come in," Karen replied. He sat down next to her on the bed.

"I knew she was going to do this, Grandpa. I could feel it," Karen said. "I'm embarrassed. Howard's gonna leave me now, just like all the other guys."

"I can't imagine the pain you're experiencing about your biological parents," her grandfather said, "and the hurt that still lingers in your heart."

"Now you understand why I wanted to move far, far away from here," Karen said.

"Holding onto anger and disappointment isn't the way to live your best Christian life. Remember Ephesians 4:31?

'Get rid of all bitterness, rage, and anger... be kind and compassionate to one another, forgiving each other, just as Christ God forgave you.'

Chapter 9

"Your biological parents must have had good reasons for choosing a closed adoption, even if we will never know why. Therefore, the best path is to forgive them. Your mom and dad have always tried to be there for you, but this is something you'll need to work through with God, Karen. Facing these feelings can be tough, but it's an important step in your healing process."

Karen sat quietly, the familiar weight on her chest tightening as she listened to her grandfather's gentle reasoning. He was right; she needed to confront her demons. And deep down, she knew that one day, she *would*. But Olga's dismissal of Karen's request to keep quiet cut deep. In the past, she would have run away: *She can't hurt me if I'm not there*. But with Howard there, she had no choice but to stay.

"I will go back out there, but Howard and I are leaving tomorrow morning. Can we come see you before we leave?" she asked.

"Of course you can," he said. "Why don't you come over at 8 a.m., and we'll have breakfast together."

"All right," Karen stood up and looked at her grandfather. He stood up, and they shared a hug.

"Let's go."

Chapter 10

When Karen's grandfather left the table, and the soft knock echoed down the hall, Howard's gaze gravitated to Olga. She sat perfectly still, her back ramrod straight, her jaw subtly clenched, with eyes fixed on an indistinguishable spot on the wall as if willing it to crack. Porter's fingers found hers, a gentle, unspoken offering of comfort.

"Don't touch me," she snapped, retracting her hand. She stood up and started taking dishes into the kitchen.

"Howard," Porter said. "I'm sorry about all this."

"On the way to Rockford, she admitted to me she was adopted. In my opinion, I believe she hates her birth parents. She doesn't hate you or Olga. She's just projecting her anger onto Olga."

Porter nodded thoughtfully, his brow furrowed as he contemplated Howard's words. "You're right," he acknowledged, his voice laced with an old weariness. "The therapists mentioned that as well."

Howard listened to the soft clinking of porcelain in the kitchen. "There are more things you should be aware of, too," Porter continued, his tone turning more serious.

An unsettling sense of dread washed over Howard. *Just how little do I truly understand about Karen?*" he thought. He fixed his gaze on Porter as Olga reappeared, collecting more dirty dishes from the table.

"Karen was a difficult teenager. When she began attending Rockford West, she started down a destructive path. She started smoking and drinking every Friday and Saturday night. When she got her driver's license, she would steal our car after we went to bed and not return till the wee hours of the morning."

"Tell him about the Sunday school class," Olga said, sitting back down in her chair.

"I told you she taught Sunday school to preschoolers at her grandfather's church in Durand," Porter said.

"Yes, I remember. If I recall, one of her students talked to her after the Christmas service," Howard replied.

"Most Saturdays, Karen partied until dawn, and by Sunday morning, she was exhausted. She struggled to teach her preschool classes. On occasion, she didn't

Chapter 10

even change clothes, smelling like alcohol and cigarettes at church. After a few months, we could see the toll it was taking on her body, and some of the parents began to feel uncomfortable having her as a teacher. We prayed for help to get her past this period in her life, but it wasn't enough.

"One Sunday morning, we woke her up for church. She refused to get out of bed, saying she had a stomachache and couldn't go to church."

Olga added, "I insisted that she go to church. I wanted to teach her a lesson—that she couldn't be responsible if she parties all night."

"Well, anyway," Porter continued. "I noticed she had bruises all over her arms; then I noticed a bruise on her face. I asked her about them, and she replied that she had fallen.

"Later that day, one of the preschool students complained to her mother that the teacher yelled at her and the other students. Her grandfather replaced Karen with another teacher, citing health problems," Porter's voice started to waiver. "But everyone in the church knew she had been assaulted."

Olga began to cry, and Porter grasped her hand. He cleared his throat and went on, "After she lost her position at the church, she distanced herself even further. Some weekdays, she'd return home around nine or ten and head straight to bed. On weekends, there were times she wouldn't come home at all. One weekend, she took the car on Friday night and did not return until Sunday. I tried to help by doing homework with her, but her grades started to suffer. We asked her to go to therapy sessions with us, and she refused. The drive to Morehead to check out Concordia College was our last father-daughter outing."

"The only things she seemed committed to were the viola and her boyfriend, John," Olga added. "Sometimes when she practiced her viola, the music was haunting and depressive. I think she found a release in her music. But she left her viola here in Rockford when she moved to Minnesota."

Howard tried to piece this together. "I think she feels abandoned by her birth parents and doesn't know where to turn. Her friends at Bailey Hall have told me she had a difficult childhood. Thank you for sharing more with me."

"Hopefully you can get through to her," Olga said. "Of all the men she's brought home, you are the most responsible and trustworthy of the lot."

The bedroom door opened, and Karen said, "Who's ready to open presents?"

Chapter 10

After a nice breakfast at her grandparents' house, they began the journey back to Minnesota.

"Now you understand why I don't like to go home much?" Karen said, glancing at Howard.

The bright sunshine reflected off the white snow as Howard reached for a pair of sunglasses. "You're right. They have many Christian values, just like my parents do."

"No, Howard, it's more than that. They are rigid and stuck in their 19th-century ways. They consider smoking, drinking, and skipping church to be sins. I know they told you I was a terrible person throughout high school, and from their perspective, I was. But I wasn't any different from the other students at West Rockford. You believe me, don't you?"

"Of course I do."

"Good," she replied, "Good."

The stark repetition of white fields and passing billboards lulled them both into a contemplative state, giving Howard a vast mental canvas on which to paint the possibilities—and the burdens—of his future. That evening, they pulled up to Comstock Hall. After dropping her off, he sought the familiar comforts of the fraternity for some much-needed sleep.

The next morning, he drove down to Lake City to spend Christmas with his mom and dad. There were two ways to get home. One road, heading straight down Highway 61 toward Lake City, was the traditional way to get home. The concrete road was straight and smooth. However, there was an alternative way. One had to turn off Highway 61 in Red Wing and take the back roads to Sugarloaf Pass. Howard knew he always had to pay attention and couldn't drive too fast on the dirt roads. In the winter, it became even more difficult since some roads were gravel and not cleared of snow. As his mind reflected on the past few days, he kept coming back to the same question: *Should I take the traditional way or take the other way?*

As he hit the outskirts of Red Wing, he'd made up his mind.

As he pulled into the driveway, a pickup truck was parked near the barn. The side of the door read, 'Reid's Veterinarian Services.' His parents told him they impregnated Bessie last spring, and she was near term. *She's probably in labor now*, he thought. Howard knew they would need help, so he headed straight to the house to change into work clothes.

Chapter 10

"Hi, Mom," Howard called out. His mother was focused on making supper, stirring a pot on the stove.

"Oh Howard, I'm glad you're here!" she replied. There was an assortment of canned tomatoes, corn, and peas on the counter. A pot roast was soaking in the sink. "You need to go out and help your father. Dr. Reid is here."

"Yes, I saw his truck. How are you doing?"

"Fine. How was Illinois? Did you have fun?"

He thought about what to say. "It went fine," he responded. "Her parents are very nice."

"Good. Now get changed and help your father."

Howard remembered when Bessie was born. He was a junior in high school. Dr. Reid had assisted with her birth, too. Howard walked into the barn and found Bessie lying on her side, with Dr. Reid attending to her.

"Good to see you, son," his dad said. "She's been in stage one for about five hours now."

"Hi, Howard! Nice to see you! Are you here for Christmas?" Dr. Reid asked.

"Yes, I just got back from Illinois yesterday and drove down from the Cities today."

After a long labor, Bessie had a beautiful baby calf. After a midnight supper with Dr. Reid, they decided to have their Christmas on a different night.

In the wee hours of the night, Howard couldn't sleep, his eyes tracing patterns on the ceiling. His thoughts kept returning to the marvel of the farm's newest addition. He remembered Bessie's birth when he was a junior. He whispered a mental count of all the heifers born in the barn. "One, two, three, four," he breathed, each number a thread connecting him to the farm's very pulse. These births, he knew, were etched into a farmer's soul.

Howard got up at 4 a.m. and checked in with Bessie and the new addition. Mother and daughter had made it through the first night together. He worked on the chores and headed in for breakfast around 8 a.m.

"Thanks for doing chores this morning, Howard," his dad said. "It was nice to sleep in for a change. How is Bessie doing?"

"She looks great. She has now expelled most of her water bag. The calf looks good. Have you decided on her name?"

"We haven't named her yet. We are waiting for you to name her," his mom replied.

"Why me? It's your heifer," Howard said.

Chapter 10

"One day, it's going to be yours, son." His father replied. "We think you should name her."

Howard thought for a second. "One of my favorite heifers was Nellie. Do you remember her? She died during my first year at Lincoln."

"Yes, she was born when you were very young," his mom said. "I remember it was when I was nursing you and teaching at the schoolhouse."

"Nellie it is," his father said.

Howard and his dad spent most of the day working on the tractors. His dad was overhauling the engine on the International and needed some help putting it back together.

"Remember, she's picky when it comes to engine oil. In the winter months, she prefers a 10W-30. But in the warmer months, I like to use 1H. It's not like your Ford. You shouldn't use the same oil for both tractors."

"Okay," Howard replied.

After a delightful dinner, they decided to celebrate Christmas. Howard had bought his dad a plaid shirt, and he gave his mom the dress that he and Karen picked out over Christmas in Rockford. "Karen thought this would look nice on you," Howard told her. "She said you deserve something nice."

One of Howard's gifts came in a large manila envelope. As his fingers broke the seal, a palpable tension filled the air; his parents watched him with rapt attention.

"Merry Christmas, Son," his father announced, his voice thick with unmistakable pride as Howard carefully slid out the document.

The once-crisp paper had softened with age, its edges worn, and the parchment itself had taken on a deep, faded yellow hue, a testament to the passage of time and generations. Prominently displayed at the top, written in large, ornate lettering, was the single, powerful word: "Deed." Howard's gaze dropped to the bottom, his breath catching in his throat. His grandfather's flowing signature was dated March 23, 1885. Below it, his own father's hand had signed on February 1, 1928. Then, a new line, starkly modern, bore his name.

Howard carefully put the document back into the manila folder. *I've dreamed of this moment for years*, he thought.

"Well, your mom and I are officially retiring. Thanks to Lake City Bank, we finally saved enough to move on to our next chapter."

Chapter 10

"We want to travel, Howard, while we are still able," his mother said. "Before you were born and we took over the farm from your grandparents, we traveled everywhere. We want to explore more of Europe and the Middle East, but we need somebody to care for the farm. We would like you to take over the farm after you graduate."

His father continued. "We've put some money down on a lakeside lot in town. In the spring, we're going to break ground. We expect to have the house finished by the end of the summer, and then you and Karen can move in."

Howard stared at the manila envelope. It was his now. All he had to do was say 'yes.'

"You're ready to take the reins, Howard. I have lots of confidence in you. And your grandfather would be proud."

Howard shook his head. "I need to think about it."

His father's expression changed into one of astonishment; his eyebrows arched, and his mouth was slightly agape. "What's there to think about, son? We're entrusting you with the farm; it's yours," he declared, his voice a mix of pride and urgency.

"Dad, when you took over the farm from Grandpa 40 years ago, times were different. All you needed was

Chapter 10

a tractor and ambition. It was a lucrative business. Today, equipment has become much more expensive. Today's farmers have to mortgage their property to make ends meet. Remember how expensive my Ford tractor was when you bought it?"

"Yes, I agree that the costs have increased. My dad said the same thing when I bought the farm; he couldn't believe the International was $850."

"And just look at the Wohlers. Due to the low future prices for corn now, they accumulated so much debt that they had to sell the farm. Today, Dick is going to be a pastor and move to Missouri, while his brothers will probably work at the grain elevator in town for the rest of their lives. Do you think their dad wanted that for his sons? Do you want that for my future?"

"Well," his dad thought for a moment. "What about your little cattle farming idea? There would be a large initial cost, but it might be more profitable for you..."

Howard shook his head. "There are other things to consider, too."

"Such as?" his mother said sharply.

"The farm is always the priority," Howard said, looking at his mother.

"Yes, of course," his father replied. "Every decision I've made has always prioritized the farm's best interests."

"Yes, that's exactly it," Howard said, pointing at his dad. "One of the biggest days of my life was graduating from high school."

"Howard, we discussed this," his mother hissed.

"You can't blame me for equipment malfunctions," his dad added. "I needed your help. Are you still mad at me about that?"

"That's just one example of how a farm can rule your life. No vacations. No time off. And no graduation ceremony. The farm always takes priority. I'm not sure I want that for myself or to force this life upon my children."

"You had a good childhood, Howard," his mother proudly said. "We raised you right. And you'll do the same for our grandkids here."

Howard paused, taking a moment to gather his thoughts as he felt the pressure of his parents' stare. "Karen shared something profound with me on our second date," he began, his voice barely above a whisper as he choked back tears. "She told me that I lacked feelings and was emotionally immature. I didn't like the sound of that."

Howard took a deep breath. "That comment—it haunted me all summer, Mom." His voice was tight and strained. "Now, I see why. You gave me so many tools for navigating life, but expressing my feelings wasn't

Chapter 10

one of them. Since last fall, she has been teaching me how to express my feelings. I've grown a lot."

His mother's brow furrowed. "What are you saying, Howard? Are you suggesting we didn't show you how to express your feelings?" Her voice was level, but a slight tremor betrayed the hurt beneath.

"Feelings are a luxury you can't have on a farm, Mom. The farm always comes first. Don't like getting up at 4 a.m.? Too bad. Is your back tired from sitting on a tractor all day? Are you bored looking at miles of corn stalks? Suck it up. We don't talk about our feelings because we *can't*. So, yes," he stated, his gaze unwavering. "Yes, I am. And honestly, this just proves the point about the farm always being the priority."

"Howard," his mother said, her voice strained, "I don't know what that woman is teaching you, but... we love you." She stood abruptly, her face hard and stern, staring out at the blackness beyond the bay window. A beat of silence hung in the air before she continued, her voice sharp with suppressed emotion. "She talked you out of owning this farm, didn't she?"

His father surged upright in his easy chair, his voice booming. "Howard, open your eyes! Can't you see she's trying to alienate you from us? She's filling your head with nonsense, pulling you away from everything you've ever wanted! You have talked about owning this farm all your life," he paused, shaking his head. "End this. She's not a good fit for this farm. or for us. This farm is your future, son."

Howard locked eyes with his father. "I'm not going to end my relationship with her. We rely on each other. She's helped me see things in a different light. And that's worth fighting for."

He handed the manila folder to his father. "Karen is my future."

Chapter 11

Karen took off her jacket and placed it behind her chair. She sat down, added a spoonful of sugar and some creamer, and stirred her coffee. The SPSC was relatively quiet today.

"Thanks for meeting me here, Patty," Karen said.

"No problem! It's good to see you," she replied. "How is life on the West Bank?"

"Being anywhere on campus—classes, the library, Coffman Union—takes under five minutes. It saves so much time. There are so many options for dining, nightlife, and activities. Honestly, if I were a freshman, I wouldn't know how to manage my time! I love the library—you can always find a nice, quiet corner to study."

"Sounds like you like it over there."

"The West Bank has such an awesome energy—it's like a different school compared to the East Bank! The Saint Paul side is much more laid-back. Looking back, I wish I had lived on the West Bank for my freshman and sophomore years and then moved to the East Bank for junior and senior years. I did this all wrong, Patty!"

"How are things going with Howard?" she asked.

Karen's tone changed as she clutched her coffee with both hands. "I don't know, Patty."

"What happened?"

"We went to see my parents in Rockford over the Christmas break. He dropped me off the day after Christmas. That's the last I heard from him."

"Karen, that was only a week ago."

"I know, but we used to chat on the phone daily before we left for Illinois."

"Well, that's strange. Did something happen?"

"My mother made a scene at Christmas dinner," Karen said with a sarcastic smile.

"Again!" Patty said. "What did she say this time?"

"She said I need to stop blaming her for the closed adoption. Right in front of Howard."

"What did you say?"

"Nothing. I took the high ground and walked away."

"Good for you!"

"During our drive home, Howard and I talked about what happened. He mentioned they had good Christian values like his parents, but that's about it. It's been over a week, and I can't help but feel he sees my struggle to

Chapter 11

forgive my biological parents as a flaw." Karen stopped and looked inside her coffee mug for inspiration. "Patty, you know I'm messed up in the head. Where did I go wrong here? He's going to break up with me, I know it!"

"First of all, stop ruminating! You're worried about things you cannot control, Karen."

"You're right," Karen said, nodding in agreement. "You said that to me before when we lived together."

"If I were in your shoes, I'd shift my focus away from the negative. Instead, I would work on the underlying issue: finding a way to forgive your birth parents. These trust issues have plagued you all your life. Think about it—you harbor all this bitterness when somebody doesn't treat you right or you feel cheated or hurt—what if you were able to let go of that bitterness and choose forgiveness instead?"

"You sound exactly like my grandpa. Okay. How do I do that?"

"Well, let me give you an example. Do you remember the incident with Michael at the sports bar after his last game of the season?"

Karen thought for a moment. "I remember being angry because he was watching some baseball game on TV with his friends when he was supposed to be joining us. I confronted him about that, and he just ignored me."

"We were having a great time, but you kept insisting Michael had to join us. Michael was clearly enjoying himself with his friends, yet you would not let it go."

"Okay," Karen said. "How would you have handled that differently?"

"Let him have a good time with his friends!"

Karen shook her head in disbelief. "But he made a plan to see us after the game?"

Patty shrugged. "So what! He is a person, and he's allowed to change his mind. He wanted to do something else. When you continued to confront him, you disrespected yourself in front of all his fraternity brothers. Then what happened?"

Karen closed her eyes and wished for a do-over. "A group of girls walked in, and he smiled and called out to one of them."

"And what did you do?"

"I got angry and said the wrong thing. Then I insisted that we leave."

"And what should you have said to him?"

"I'm angry that you didn't join us, and I'm bitter that you thought she's prettier than me."

Chapter 11

Patty smiled. "Good! That's acknowledging your bitterness to someone who did you wrong. Now, why did you get angry?"

"He didn't do what he said he was going to do."

"Deeper."

Karen thought for a second, then the light came on. "I didn't trust him."

"Bingo. That's a reflection on why you reacted the way you did. Now, how can you let go of this anger and forgive?"

"I allowed my lack of trust to poison the whole situation. Then I exploded." She stared at the wall as the pieces of the puzzle began to click into place. "It was never about him, was it? It was always about me. I need to find a way to forgive myself for letting my lack of trust in others get the better of me."

Patty took a sip of her coffee. "It's a three-step process: acknowledgment, reflection, and forgiveness. Understanding your feelings can be challenging, especially when someone hurts you openly like Michael did. It makes you feel vulnerable, and you want to run away."

"Yeah," Karen agreed.

"Now, I want you to consider how you can forgive your mother and your biological parents. The answers may not come easily, like what happened with Michael at the bar, but over time, you will find your way. Don't forget to acknowledge what happened, reflect on why it occurred, and forgive."

She continued. "There's another great reason to talk to someone who has hurt you. When you share your feelings, you strengthen the trust of the relationship, and that trust adds up over time," Patty said. "A long time ago, my mom shared this idea with me about an emotional bank account. In a relationship, we make emotional deposits by being vulnerable and open with each other. But, if we don't express our feelings or try to avoid the issue, it's like making a withdrawal. It's important to keep a positive balance in our relationships."

"Wow! How come you never told me this idea before?" Karen asked. "I could've saved my relationship with Michael."

"Well, maybe," Patty said. "Your relationship with Michael was superficial at best. You two looked so cute together, but that's all you had. He had a wandering eye."

"But what about Howard? He's seen the ugly side of me and my family now. Did he give up on me?"

"What did I just tell you about Michael when he didn't want to sit with us at the sports bar?"

Chapter 11

"He is a person, and he is allowed to change his mind."

"Exactly. And we know that he plans to take over the family farm after graduating from college. Are you prepared to work on a farm for the rest of your life?"

"But he mentioned that he might not do that."

"Honey, listen. You can take the farmer out of the farm, but you can't take the farm out of the farmer."

She was right. "Patty, I can't work on a farm."

"So, there's your answer. Maybe this confrontation with your mother in front of Howard was a good thing. It made it a nice, clean cut."

"But I've invested so much time in him, Patty," Karen murmured, her gaze unfocused, searching for words. "Look, I don't always feel fireworks when we are together, but he's this comforting weight, like a warm blanket on a cold winter night. It's so easy with him. Don't you think that counts as—genuine love?"

"Then it's time to trade in your manis and your Mary Quant dresses for dirty fingernails and overalls, dear."

Comstock Hall's lobby wasn't just a place; it was a vibrant hub. The tink-tink-tink of ping-pong balls echoed through the game room, while others were lost in board game battles. Walter Cronkite's voice emanated from the television room. The sitting area boasted plush, new sofas, whose fabric emitted the subtle, almost sweet scent of fresh upholstery. This space dwarfed Bailey Hall's, a modern haven compared to its older sibling. Karen sank into one of the inviting chairs, her gaze drifting over the energetic ping-pong players.

Occasionally, she glanced at the entrance, waiting for him to arrive and pick her up. He'd actually called and asked her to dinner! A thrill coursed through her, but a whisper of doubt lingered: *What if this is the last time?*

She thought back to Christmas. *Why did my mother have to act that way in front of Howard?* she thought. *Because she was upset that I had blamed her for the closed adoption. I brought this on myself.* She sighed and shook her head. Her timing couldn't have been worse, though, and now she was on the verge of losing a great guy.

How do you forgive somebody for that? she wondered. Patty had suggested using 'I feel' statements to help cope with the negative thoughts that arose in her mind.

I feel angry that she made a scene during Christmas dinner.

Chapter 11

I feel terrible for the way I treated her all these years.

Karen let out a sigh and looked over at the entrance where a group of nuns was heading out for the evening. *Maybe I should become a nun*, she thought.

She rose and gazed outside at the torrent of students pouring down University Avenue. Their excited shouts and laughter sliced through the frigid evening air. Most of them were heading for Mariucci Arena to watch the Saturday night hockey game. Puffs of their breath plumed like miniature clouds as they surged past, a vibrant wave of maroon and gold.

Howard stood beside her. "Great view."

Karen acted surprised. "Oh! I didn't see you come in."

"The check-in desk told me you were over here. Are you ready for supper?"

Karen smiled. "Let's go!" She grabbed her jacket and signed out as they braved the cold January night for his Beetle.

No kiss? she thought. *This is bad. And he's not saying much. Maybe I should say how I feel.*

"I missed you," she blurted out as they were walking.

He looked over and smiled. "I missed you, too."

"Where are we going?" she inquired as he opened her car door.

Howard smiled as he closed her door and walked around the front of his car. *He really isn't saying much, is he?*

"Howard, why are you teasing me like this? Where are we going?" she asked again as they drove down University Avenue. Once more, he responded with silence and a smile.

He pulled into a dark drive-in restaurant and turned off the car. "What are we doing here?" she inquired. "Drive-ins are closed in January."

"Do you remember this place, Karen?" he asked.

Her gaze swept over the deserted drive-in, a silent, dark shell in the winter night. Only the streetlights offered enough illumination to outline its forgotten shape. The barest whisper of drive-in food hung in the chill, a memory carried on the wind, and then, like a sudden chill itself, it struck her.

"Yeah, now I do. We came here to eat in that old car on our first date," she said, looking at Howard. "But it's the middle of winter, and they're shut down. We can't eat here!"

"We're not eating in the car. Come on, let's go!" he said, going around to open the door for her.

As they rushed to the employee entrance, the rich, smoky aroma of charbroiled burgers and the salty tang

Chapter 11

of hot French fries intensified, drawing them forward with an almost magnetic pull.

"Hello?" Howard called out after they went inside. "Junior?"

"Hold up," a man yelled from the back room. As they removed their jackets, he came through the swing doors wearing a chef's uniform.

"Well, hey, y'all," he drawled, his voice a rich, warm cadence that felt as warm as Georgia sunshine. "You must be Karen. Heard tell quite a bit 'bout you."

"Karen, this is my fraternity brother, Junior."

"Earl is my given name, ma'am. But only my mama call me dat when I'm fitin' to get a whippin'. My pa's name, it was Earl, too, so I goes by Junior."

Karen's mouth curved into a bewildered smile. Never in a million years could she have expected this. "What in the world is going on here?" she asked.

"I'm whippin' up a real nice meal. Y'all like cheeseburgers and fries, ain't 'cha?"

"Junior works here part-time as a chef during the season. We talked to the owner, and they let us use the restaurant for the evening."

Junior looked at Karen. "Speak the gospel truth, now—rumor has it he took you to this greasy spoon for y'all's first date?"

"Yes, he did," Karen replied, looking at Howard.

Chapter 11

"And you still with him?" He looked at Howard. "Common sense ain't a flower that grows in everyone's garden," he laughed and slapped Howard on the back. "Look here, you be as pretty as a Georgia peach. If you ever want to meet a nice, respectable southern gentleman, look my way."

Karen blushed and laughed. "I'll keep it in mind."

Junior pointed to the break room booth. "Now, y'all just sit comfy like over there 'n Junior gonna take good care a' ya, hear?" He turned and walked back through the swing doors as they took a seat.

"Junior is a new pledge this year. His parents own a cotton and bean farm near Albany, Georgia."

"How does he like all this snow and cold weather?"

"Well, it's his first winter in Minneapolis. He really likes the snow, but he hates the cold."

They sat there for a few seconds. Karen decided to make an emotional deposit.

"Howard, I want to be honest with you. I often feel a wave of jealousy when I see you spending time with other women. It makes me question whether I'm truly good enough for someone like you. I know these feelings of insecurity and trust are rooted in my teenage years back in Illinois because my biological parents abandoned me. Unfortunately, I get these feelings when I see you with other women."

Howard reached across the table, his hand gently covering Karen's. "It takes courage to admit that," Howard said, his gaze warm and steady. "Forgiveness, especially of yourself, is a long journey, particularly when past hurts run deep. I'm proud of you. Do you trust me?"

"Yes, I do," she whispered, her fingers curling around his.

"Trust is something that is built piece by piece, every single day," he continued. "Has the trust you've placed in me started to quiet those jealous feelings when other women talk to me? Is it making a difference for you?"

"Sometimes, but most of the time, no."

"How can you help yourself when this happens?"

"Telling you how I feel and telling myself that I still trust you and forgive you," she replied.

"Good. If you can learn to forgive yourself when you feel jealousy, it's a good first step towards learning forgiveness of both your mom and your birth parents."

"Can I ask you a question? Are you mad at me for what happened in Rockford?"

"Of course not!"

Karen breathed a sigh of relief. "But you have been so quiet lately?"

Chapter 11

Junior came through the swing doors with two baskets. "Two cheeseburgers with fries," he proclaimed and set them down. "Cokes okay with y'all?"

They both agreed, and Junior returned with two glasses of soda. "Dig in!"

"Thanks, Junior!" Howard said as he disappeared into the kitchen.

Karen took a small bite of the cheeseburger and ate a French fry, waiting for his response.

"Karen, I've been interviewing for jobs with banks. On Thursday, I interviewed with the Federal Home Loan Bank."

Karen's heart leapt. *He is still considering working in a bank instead of on the farm.* "How did it go?"

"I wasn't that impressed. They don't seem very organized, and they don't seem interested in me."

"Their loss," Karen said, smiling at Howard and biting another French fry.

"On Monday, I have an interview with a government agency called the Farmers Home Administration. Maybe that one will go better."

Was he truly abandoning the farm idea now? His lifelong aspiration? She aimed for casualness when she finally broke the silence. "So, what are your plans after graduation?" she asked, taking a sip of Coke.

"It's still too early to tell. Hopefully, I can find something here in the Twin Cities and be close to you."

"What about the farm?"

Howard glanced down at the half-eaten cheeseburger and fries in the green woven basket, as if the answers lie in their greasy depths. His raw gaze finally met Karen's. "Before you," Howard began, "all my dreams were just... the farm. I never thought to stop and think what I wanted, because the farm was all I knew." He leaned forward, staring hard into her eyes. "But after our first date here, you've completely rewired how I see the world. You've woken up ideas and dreams that were unknown. And since Illinois..." Howard paused, "Karen, it's not just that I need you in my life. It's that life doesn't make sense without you."

Howard exhaled slowly, the weight of his thoughts reflected in his weary expression. "After I dropped you off, I went home for Christmas," he began. "We were opening presents, and they... told me they're ready to retire." He ran a hand through his hair. "Karen, my dad gave me the deed. It's mine. The farm. The moment I've waited for my whole life."

Karen's heart dropped. *Please, no!* The happy mask she wore felt fragile. *I love him so much, but I can't live that life, his life.* With a shaky breath, she manufactured a smile. "Wow, congratulations!" she exclaimed, her voice chirpy. "That's great!"

Chapter 11

Howard paused. A heavy silence fell between them. "Well, I turned it down. I explained to them that farming just isn't feasible for a small operation like ours anymore, not in the 1960s." He shifted, avoiding her gaze.

Karen managed, "Oh my," her voice and face carefully neutral. But inside, her spirit soared with pure, unrestrained elation.

"They were angry. My mom even said, 'You chose Karen over the family.'" He glanced into her eyes, frowning as he recalled their anger. "A few weeks ago, they bought some land in Lake City. They plan to build a house there in the spring and travel around the world."

"What are they going to do?" Karen asked, concern creeping into her voice.

"I don't know," he admitted, looking at his half-eaten cheeseburger. "But that's their problem now."

The raw storm of emotions contorted his face. His lips formed a tight line, and his brow furrowed deeper than ever. But as compassion and admiration washed over her, Karen reached across the table, taking his hands and intertwining their greasy fingers once more. It was a silent offering of warmth and steadfast support. A tender smile blossomed on her face, chasing away some of the room's lingering heaviness and a fraction of the burden from his shoulders. "You gave up your dream for me," she whispered. Her voice was a delicate blend of awe and sorrow. "No one has ever made such a sacrifice for me." Leaning forward, she gave him a soft, sweet kiss.

"The dream I had of running the farm was not my dream—it was my family's. It took me some time to figure that out. But you help me make the right decision."

One of the swing doors creaked open, and Junior's head peeked out, his deep Georgia drawl cutting through their dwindling chatter. "Y'all 'bout done? I's gonna start closin' things down here." His gaze, sharp and assessing, swept over their table.

Howard caught Karen's eye, a fleeting, shared understanding passing between them. "Yeah, we're done here," he confirmed.

Karen turned towards Junior. "Thank you for dinner, Junior." She glanced back at Howard, then added, "We had a great time."

As the words left her lips, Junior was already efficiently gathering their empty baskets and Coke glasses. Howard and Karen shrugged into their winter

Chapter 11

jackets. Their bodies bracing, almost instinctively, for the biting January night that awaited them.

They scrambled for the Beetle, chivalry be damned, as they each fumbled with their icy door handles. Once inside, even protected by metal and glass, the biting north wind still stung their cheeks and fingers. Howard fired the engine, the familiar **doof-doof-doof** rattling to life, but instead of driving away, Howard sat for a few seconds, lost in thought. Karen listened to the engine's rhythmic thrum, shivering and willing the car to warm the cabin faster. The silence stretched, filled only by the Beetle's mechanical rhythm and the distant howl of the wind outside. Finally, he turned, a small, weary smile breaking through his expression.

"Karen," Howard murmured, "Our childhoods were rough for both of us. Our families, our challenges... but with you, I feel like we can overcome anything. We are stronger, together," he said, his voice warm and reassuring. "There will be more challenges ahead, but I can't imagine anyone else I'd rather have by my side to solve them." He opened the glove compartment and took out a small box.

Karen's mind reeled. *This is it? Here? Now?* She was huddled in a rumbling Beetle, smelling exhaust fumes and feeling the Arctic chill of a desolate January evening at a locked-up drive-in in Minnesota. But soon a slow, unstoppable warmth began to spread through her. *It isn't what I imagined,* she thought, a joyous smile finally breaking through. *It's even better.*

Epilogue

Like many marriages, Karen and Howard's relationship had its share of ups and downs, but through it all, they always returned to the core principles of a strong marriage: effort, commitment, trust, and open communication.

It's become a cherished tradition that every August 21st, Howard expresses his love for Karen in his own slightly goofy way, teasing, "I think I'll keep you around for another year."

Karen and Howard celebrated their 60th wedding anniversary on August 21st, 2025.

About the Author

A non-fiction author and novelist, Lisa Boatman is renowned for her ability to craft page-turning stories brimming with intricate plots and multifaceted characters. Drawing on a diverse upbringing that included the Mid-South, East Coast, and Upper Midwest, her writing offers a distinctive perspective, fusing narrative history with a locational lens.

Lisa lives in Lisbon, Portugal.

www.ingramcontent.com/pod-product-compliance
Lightning Source LLC
Chambersburg PA
CBHW020453030426
42337CB00011B/101